The Kennedys: The Lives and Legacies of John, Jackie, Robert, and Ted Kennedy

By Charles River Editors

About Charles River Editors

Charles River Editors was founded by Harvard and MIT alumni to provide superior editing and original writing services, with the expertise to create digital content for publishers across a vast range of subject matter. In addition to providing original digital content for third party publishers, Charles River Editors republishes civilization's greatest literary works, bringing them to a new generation via ebooks.

Visit charlesrivereditors.com for more information.

Introduction

John F. Kennedy (1917-1963)

In many ways, John Fitzgerald Kennedy and his young family were the perfect embodiment of the '60s. The decade began with a sense of idealism, personified by the attractive Kennedy, his beautiful and fashionable wife Jackie, and his young children. Months into his presidency, Kennedy exhorted the country to reach for the stars, calling upon the nation to send a man to the Moon and back by the end of the decade. In 1961, Kennedy made it seem like anything was possible, and Americans were eager to believe him. The Kennedy years were fondly and famously labeled "Camelot," by Jackie herself, suggesting an almost mythical quality about the young President and his family.

As it turned out, the '60s closely reflected the glossy, idealistic portrayal of John F. Kennedy, as well as the uglier truths. The country would achieve Kennedy's goal of a manned moon mission, and the landmark Civil Rights Act of 1964 finally guaranteed minorities their civil rights and restored equality, ensuring that the country "would live out the true meaning of its creed." But the idealism and optimism of the decade was quickly shattered, starting with Kennedy's assassination in 1963. The '60s were permanently marred by the Vietnam War, and by the time Robert F. Kennedy and Martin Luther King, Jr. were assassinated in 1968, the country was irreversibly jaded. The events of the decade produced protests and countercultures unlike anything the country had seen before, as young people came of age more quickly than ever.

The Kennedys humanizes the nation's youngest elected president, explaining the roots of the Kennedy family, the basis for John's presidential ambitions, his war service and journalism, his political career and assassination, and all of the accomplishments and shortcomings inbetween. Along the way, you will learn interesting facts about JFK you never knew, like which famous relative also died on November 22, and see pictures of the important people and events in his life.

Jacqueline Kennedy Onassis (1929-1994)

In 1961, President John F. Kennedy made it seem like anything was possible, and Americans were eager to believe him. The next three years would be fondly and famously labeled "Camelot," suggesting an almost mythical quality about the young President and his family. The famous label came from John's fashionable and beautiful wife, Jackie, whose elegance and grace made her the most popular woman in the world. Her popularity threatened to eclipse even her husband's, who famously quipped on one presidential trip to France that he was "the man who accompanied Jacqueline Kennedy to Paris."

Americans were fascinated by the young First Lady's style, and the manner in which she glamorously positioned both the First Family and the White House in those years, and Jackie remains one of the country's most popular First Ladies. But it was in the face of adversity that she truly made her lasting mark, with the country taking its cue from her in the aftermath of the president's assassination. Having devised and lit the eternal flame at JFK's tombstone, Jackie also set about securing her husband's legacy, a time still fondly and mythically remembered as Camelot today, despite his legendary transgressions and infidelities.

Jackie continued to fascinate Americans over the next several decades, acting as a living symbol of the Kennedy years and a popular unofficial representative for her country abroad. She famously went on to marry Greek shipping magnate Aristotle Onassis, earning her the nickname Jackie O, and she took up a career in publishing beginning in the mid-70s. Until her death in 1994, even in her 60s she continued to be the subject of popular interest and intense tabloid and paparazzi coverage.

The Kennedys details the fame and fashion of the famous First Lady, while also examining her legacy during and after her years in the White House.

Robert F. Kennedy (1925-1968)

In some ways, Robert Francis Kennedy (1925–1968) is the quintessential middle brother among the Kennedys, eclipsed in life while working in his brother John's administration, eclipsed in death both by his older brother's assassination and his younger brother's long, influential career in the Senate as a liberal lion. And yet, the politics of the 1960s and the ultimate legacy of the Kennedys, including the "Kennedy Curse", would have been incomplete without Bobby's place in the narrative.

As Bobby's private life and public life played out, the two came to mirror each other. Among the Kennedy clan, Bobby remained within the shadow of older brothers Joseph Jr. and John, both of whom their father thought were destined to become political scions. And ultimately, it was Ted who cast the longest political shadow, serving for decades in government. But Bobby may have been the most intellectual and ideological of them all. And it was Bobby who worked behind the scenes to help advance John's political career, including his political campaigns and as Attorney General in his administration.

Eventually, with the deaths of his brothers, Bobby rose to become the leader of the Kennedy family, at the same time his political prominence rose. Today, unfortunately, Bobby is best remembered for his assassination, the way in which it helped perpetuate the "Kennedy Curse", and the fact that his political promise, including potentially becoming president in 1968, was never fulfilled.

The Kennedys looks at Bobby's place in the political and cultural narrative of the Kennedys and the 1960s, but it also humanizes the middle brother who labored tirelessly for the good of his family, the ideological advocate who took courageous stands, and the man who juggled the demands of being a Kennedy with his own political ambitions.

Edward "Ted" Kennedy (1932-2009)

When Edward Kennedy was born in 1932, he was the youngest sibling in a family destined to produce some of America's most influential political leaders. By the time he was a teenager, his oldest brother, Joseph Kennedy Jr., had died a war hero, his brother John was on the fast track to political stardom, and his brother Bobby was managing John's campaigns. Though Ted was a star athlete, his parents were more focused on his older brothers.

Ted may not have been the center of attention in the Kennedy family then or now, but he had the same charisma and skills of his older brothers, as well as the same controversial vices. And as fate would have it, Ted's political legacy may have eclipsed them all. His brothers were victims of two of the country's most tragic assassinations, two other siblings died in plane crashes, and he would have to eulogize nephews. But Ted had the extra gift of length of years, surviving his encounter with the "Kennedy Curse", a 1964 plane crash that severely injured and nearly killed him.

Although controversy ensured Ted would never be president, he spent nearly half a century in the U.S. Senate, forging a legacy that earned him the nickname "The Lion of the Senate". Indeed, in the course of becoming the 4th longest serving Senator in American history, Ted became the patriarch of both the Kennedy family and the Democratic Party, as well as one of the most forceful and outspoken advocates of progressivism. But he also held the respect of his Republican counterparts, and Ted was able to bridge political gaps in the process of authoring and sponsoring hundreds of bills that became law.

The Kennedys details Ted's life and career within the Kennedy family and the political world, including all of its famous ups and infamous downs, while also analyzing the legacy of the youngest Kennedy brother. Along with pictures of Ted and important people, places, and events in his life, you will learn about The Lion of the Senate like you never have before, in no time at all.

Chapter 1: Growing Up a Kennedy

The Kennedy Family Background

Over 50 years after the Kennedy Brothers rose to political power in the United States, the name Kennedy remains the nation's most famous political name. But to understand how each of the three Kennedy brothers got to where they did, it's essential to understand their family background, as well as each one's place within the immediate family itself.

The Kennedys were descendants of Patrick Kennedy, an Irish Catholic who immigrated to Boston from County Wexford, Ireland, in 1849, amid the Irish Potato Famine. In Boston, Patrick married another Irish immigrant named Bridget Murphy. The couple had five children, among them PJ Kennedy, Robert Kennedy's grandfather. Tragedy, however, struck the family when Patrick died of cholera on November 22nd, 1858, exactly 105 years before his great grandson, John Kennedy, was assassinated.

Afterwards, Bridget tended the family by opening a small but modestly successful stationary and liquor store. Her son, PJ Kennedy, capitalized on this liquor-selling business and became enormously wealthy. He began importing whisky, often illegally, and reaped enormous profits selling to upper class Bostonians. He owned bars throughout the city.

PJ Kennedy was the first Kennedy to enter politics, being elected five times to the Massachusetts House of Representatives and twice to the Massachusetts State Senate. Though these local political accomplishments would be greatly eclipsed by his descendants', it was P.J. who laid the groundwork for a political dynasty.

If P.J. laid the groundwork for the Kennedy family dynasty, it was son Joseph who would put it into action. Joseph Sr. certainly knew his political fortunes would be bolstered when he married Rose Fitzgerald, the daughter of Boston Mayor John F. "Honey Fitz" Fitzgerald, another member of Boston's growing Irish Catholic political elite. Together, Rose and Joseph P. Kennedy had nine children, among them John, Bobby, and Ted, all major figures in national American politics.

Joseph Kennedy Sr.

Today Joseph Sr. is best remembered as the family patriarch and the ambitious driving force that propelled his sons onto the national scene. But that reputation was not what Joseph Sr. envisioned when Ted and the others were growing up; before placing his stock in his sons, the intensely ambitious father hoped to reach the White House himself. In addition to boosting the family fortunes through investments in liquor, real estate and movies, Joseph Sr. was appointed by President Franklin Roosevelt to become the first chairman of the Securities and Exchange Commission (SEC), a department created by the New Deal to combat illicit investment. Although it is still unclear whether Joseph Sr. engaged in any illegal importation of alcohol during Prohibition, it was widely believed that he was a crook, and when asked why he would select such a man to chair the SEC and combat fraud, President Roosevelt replied, "It takes one to catch one."

Throughout this time, Joseph Sr.'s standing within the Democratic Party as a whole continued to rise, and he reached his political peak when Roosevelt selected him to be the war-time Ambassador to Great Britain, the United States' most important World War II ally. By now, he had his sights set on the White House himself.

Joseph Sr.'s political ambitions would be dashed by his own controversial stances. During the war, one in which he was serving as an ambassador to a country fighting for its survival, he was something of a defeatist, having repeatedly argued that the war was futile, that Hitler would dominate Europe, and that democracy in England and the United States might cease to exist. Joseph Sr. also became increasingly isolationist, arguing that affairs in Europe were unrelated to American international prominence, and that the defense of Britain was not done in the name of democracy, but only in the interest of British national self-preservation. Although there were many isolationists at the time, and son John was partly associated with the America First Committee, Roosevelt strongly opposed those views and removed Kennedy from the position of Ambassador to Great Britain. Of course, isolationism was bombed right along with Pearl Harbor on December 7, 1941.

Kennedy's demotion from his post and the aftermath during the war destroyed all hopes of a further political career. When the full horrors of the Holocaust became clear, information was leaked that indicated Joseph Sr. had actually thought that Nazi genocide against the Jews was deserved; the Jews, he thought, had brought it upon themselves. He didn't morally oppose the extermination of the Jews – he was an anti-Semite – but he merely thought the Germans should have reduced the Jews in a way that generated less negative publicity.

John's Childhood and Early Life

John F. Kennedy was always intended for greatness, or at least one male in his family was. On May 29th, 1917, John Fitzgerald Kennedy was born into a prominent Boston political family in Brookline, Massachusetts. The second son of Joseph P. Kennedy and Rose Fitzgerald, young John spent the first 10 years of his life in Brookline attending prominent private schools in the Boston area.

In 1927, the family left Massachusetts for the Bronx. While in the New York area, the Kennedy's moved around, but John remained a student at the Riverdale School in the Bronx.

Later, John's high school experience put him in one of the most elite schools in the country. Kennedy enrolled first at the Canterbury School and then later at the Choate School in Wallingford, Connecticut. This was hardly unusual for the Kennedy clan, which had enrolled many of its children at Choate, alongside some of the nation's most important political families. Choate was a member of a group of elite preparatory schools in New England, including Deerfield, Hotchkiss and St. Paul's.

After graduating from Choate in 1935, Kennedy had the opportunity to select from a list of prestigious universities. He travelled abroad to consider studying at the London School of Economics but ultimately chose to enrolled at Princeton, though only for a few weeks due to illness. He transferred to Harvard, where he remained until graduating.

In fact, illness would be one of the defining features of John's life, disrupted Kennedy's education throughout his early life. Many of his problems during this time were gastrointestinal, and he was hospitalized repeatedly to recuperate. He often spent time at his family vacation home in Hyannisport, Massachusetts, to recover.

Despite illness, Kennedy was a star student at Harvard, and he graduated on time. Although he had ties to the America First Committee, the famous isolationist group that advocated steering clear of World War II, Kennedy's undergraduate thesis focused on England's appeasement policy towards Nazi Germany, and how it had led to the outbreak of World War II. This was an important piece of scholarship, and it was later published into a book in 1940 under the title *Why England Slept*. Young Kennedy took a prominent interest in foreign affairs and was now contributing to the intellectual discussion of the topic.

Bobby's Childhood and Early Life

On November 20, 1925, Robert F. Kennedy was born in Brookline, Massachusetts, the seventh child of Joseph P. Kennedy and Rose E. Fitzgerald. By the time he was born, Bobby had become part of an important political family whose ancestors had held considerable sway in the Boston area. But Bobby's father, Joseph Kennedy, now the family patriarch, intended to create a family dynasty on a national scale.

Thus, despite the fact Boston had been a power base for both the Kennedys and Fitzgeralds dating back generations, Bobby and the rest of the children spent only a limited amount of their childhood in Massachusetts. When he was barely two years old, the Kennedy family relocated to the Bronx. Kennedy, however, was able to spend summers at his family compound in Hyannisport, Massachusetts, so his associations with Massachusetts were not completely gone.

Bobby may have had all the disadvantages of being a middle child, especially in a family so large, but as a child he was afforded one of the most affluent upbringings possible. Hailing from one of the nation's most important families, he was able to attend some of the country's most prestigious schools. As a young child, he attended public schools in Bronxville, but later attended private academies, including the Bronxville School and the Riverdale Country School. When he was 12, Joseph Kennedy became U.S. Ambassador to the United Kingdom, a position he hoped to use as a stepping stone to bigger and better things. As a result, Bobby was enrolled at the prestigious Gibbs School for Boys.

While his father stayed in Europe, the family moved back to the U.S. just before the outbreak of World War II, where Bobby went to a boarding school called St. Paul's in Concord, New Hampshire. Joseph Jr., the family's golden boy, was already of fighting age, as was older brother John, and both of them became decorated war veterans, which Joseph Sr. viewed as a crucial step in establishing his boys' political bona fides. Bobby, however, was still a teenager, and the only battles he was a part of were the ones between his parents over which prestigious school to send him to. Bobby's parents became picky about his schooling, sending him to various elite preparatory institutions until finally settling on the very prestigious Milton Academy in Massachusetts. Milton had already established an elite reputation for producing famous Americans like T.S. Eliot and helping prepare young adults for entrance into schools like Harvard.

Bobby graduated from high school amid the nation's involvement in World War II. As a young man, he was required to register for the draft, which he did. He enlisted in the US Naval Reserve, while also enrolling at Harvard University.

Ted's Childhood and Early Life

When Edward "Ted" Moore Kennedy was born to Joseph P. Kennedy and Rose Fitzgerald Kennedy on February 22, 1932, in the Dorchester section of Boston, Massachusetts, he became the youngest child in the Kennedy family. Ted was born several years after his youngest sibling, Jean, and the gap between the 9 Kennedy children meant that Joseph Jr. and John were already well into their teens before he was born. In fact, John served as Ted's Godfather.

Though the country was largely unfamiliar with the Kennedys, Ted had been born into a family intently focused on political careers. Joseph Kennedy Sr. was climbing the political ladder in a career that would eventually land him an ambassadorship, and in the 1930s he still harbored dreams of possibly running for the presidency. At the same time, he had high hopes for his boys, who he anticipated would also rise to high office. However, as the youngest of the nine Kennedy children, with 3 older brothers who excelled at everything they did, Ted's wait in line seemed certain to take awhile, if not forever. On top of that, his parents thought his elder siblings held more long-term promise.

Due in part to his father's career, Ted's education was scattered and unstable. Though he was born in Boston, he only lived there a short time. Thereafter, his family moved to Bronxville, New York, just outside of New York City. Young Ted also lived in Hyannisport, Massachusetts, and in London, where his father served as U.S. ambassador to Great Britain. Given his place in the family and his travels and travails, perhaps it's not surprising that Ted did not prove to be a star student, but regardless that fit his parents' expectations. Though he was fortunate to attend some of the nation's and world's most prestigious schools, he did not excel in them.

Due to his young age, Ted also endured the first of the Kennedy family's tragedies at a considerably younger age than John and Robert. His elder sister, Rosemary, underwent a lobotomy that left her emotionless and distant, and during World War II, when John and Joseph Jr. served with distinction, Ted was still in his early teens. It was as a teenager that Ted would have to cope with Joseph Jr.'s death in the war. Sister Kathleen was also killed in an airplane crash in 1948.

During those trying years, young Ted was fortunate to attend the Milton Academy in Massachusetts, a prestigious preparatory school. He enjoyed his time there, and it was among his most stable and consistent years of education. A star football player, Ted played on the academy's team, while also playing hockey and tennis. Ted utilized his natural social skills on the debate team and in drama as well before graduating from Milton in 1950.

The Brothers' Places within the Kennedy Family

Though each brother had a similar kind of privileged upbringing only money could buy, they each held different lots growing up within their family, which had an important effect on their early lives and their political futures.

With his own hopes reduced, Joseph Sr. invested all of his energy into pushing his sons to the forefront. Naturally, this began with the eldest sons, primarily his namesake Joseph Kennedy Jr. Before becoming a bomber pilot during World War II, Joseph Jr. was a student at Harvard Law School and had already been a delegate at the Democratic National Convention of 1940. Handsome, bright, and charming, the rest of the Kennedys looked up to their oldest brother, who was primed to become the family's political standard bearer and possibly President. Bobby would name his first born son after his oldest brother, and some of the time he did serve in the Navy was aboard the USS Joseph P. Kennedy Jr., a Navy ship that would also form part of the blockade of Cuba ordered by President John F. Kennedy.

Joseph Kennedy Jr.

Unfortunately for the family, the reason a Navy ship had been commissioned and named after Joseph Jr. was because he had been killed in combat in July 1944. Having already completed 25 missions, Joseph Jr. decided against returning home and instead took part in an experimental operation, and he was killed during the first mission of the operation when his plane exploded. He was just 29.

Joseph Jr.'s premature death rattled his brothers, but it also resulted in having the second-eldest son, John, become the family's Presidential standard-bearer. John was not a bad candidate himself, having also become a decorated war hero during the war for the manner in which he saved his crew after his PT-109 collided with a Japanese destroyer. With his elite background and military decorations, John was well on his way to political stardom, and he had the ambition to match.

It was against this backdrop that Bobby came of age. Not only was Bobby the seventh child born into the family, he was also very much the runt of the litter, considerably smaller in size and stature to his older brothers and younger brother Edward. Like Ted, Bobby faced the threat of being lost in the Kennedy crowd, and it also did not escape his notice that his father, who everyone aimed to please, was more personally invested in his older brothers.

Acutely aware of his position in the family, Bobby aimed to stand out by acting larger than life, developing a reputation for being both fiercely loyal and competitive, which curried favor with his father. Bobby let his passions drive him, becoming known as the most devout member of the family, the strongest tempered, and the hardest working. He was certainly not the first in line for family attention, but Bobby's traits were valued by his family, especially his older brother John in the wake of Joseph Jr.'s death. While helping his older brother successfully run for Congress in 1946, it was noted that Bobby worked harder on the campaign than the candidate himself.

While the status seemed to affect Bobby's work ethic and attitude, Ted seemed to have a more passive reaction to his lot in the family. Longtime Kennedy family friend Ted Sorenson recalled that Ted "did not initially seem to be much more than the 'kid brother' — fun, funny, friendly, but not a major part of the genial Kennedy dinner-table conversations on policy and politics." Obviously Ted would eventually enter politics, but even that was at the behest of his father, who had to spur him into action in the early 1960s. Throughout his early years, Ted seemed content to play the charming, popular jock. Fully recognizing his place in the family, Ted once noted, "The disadvantage of my position is being constantly compared with two brothers of such superior ability."

Chapter 2: Growing Up a Bouvier

Jackie as a child

Jackie's Birth and Childhood

Given her destiny to grow up to be one of the most graceful and beautiful women in America, it is no surprise that Jacqueline "Jackie" Bouvier would make a prominent rise and attract the notice of anybody who saw her, including an eventual president. But there were other aspects of her family background that made her the perfect woman to join the Kennedy family.

On July 28, 1929, Jackie was born into a family of wealth and affluence in Bellport, New York, a community near the affluent Hamptons area of Long Island. Jackie was born into a family of wealth and affluence. Her father, John Vernou Bouvier III, was a Wall Street stock broker, and her mother Janet Lee came from a similarly wealthy background in the New York

City area. Jackie was born two years after Joseph Kennedy Sr. had moved his family, including young sons John and Robert, to the Bronx.

The Bouvier family background was complex but uniformly wealthy. Jackie was of Irish, Scottish, English and French backgrounds, and the Bouvier children were raised as devout Roman Catholics. Although that background would later make her an ideal woman for an Irish Catholic Kennedy to marry, at the time Catholicism was still a partial stain on her family's otherwise respectable status. Tensions between Catholics and Protestants in New York City had dated back decades, during waves of Irish immigration to the city, and Democratic politics were often fractured by the religious differences. That divide had still marked a major issue even during the political rise of Franklin Delano Roosevelt less than 20 years earlier.

Nevertheless, the Bouvier family owned estates throughout the country, in upscale and wealthy locations like Newport, Rhode Island, and the Hamptons. As a child, Jackie attended the prestigious Chapin School in New York City, where she developed a fascination and intense interest in equestrian. Jackie would remain passionate about horses and riding for the rest of her life, an interest so strong and noted that Pakistani President Ayub Khan would give her a horse as a goodwill gesture while she was First Lady.

In 1940, when Jackie was only 11, her parents divorced, which was still a social taboo during the time period, especially for Catholics. As a result, Jackie and her sister Lee divided their time between their mother and father, with John remaining in New York City while Janet moved between Virginia and New England. The Bouvier father remained in New York City, while the mother moved between Virginia and New England. Her father also owned an estate called "Lasata" in the Hamptons, which he had inherited from his father, "The Major", John Bouvier Jr. Jackie spent several summers there, most notably honing her horse riding skills.

Lasata, Jackie's summer home, privately bought in 2006 at a price of $25 million.

Jackie's Education

Like her future husband, Jackie's family wealth enabled her to acquire a relatively privileged education. And though she moved around to different schools after her parents' divorce, prestige and high academic quality continued to define her education.

In 1942, Jackie's mother remarried to a wealthy Standard Oil heir named Hugh Auchincloss Jr., which improved the family's already high standard of living, and throughout the 1940's, Jackie was afforded a world class education at various academies in the Northeast, including the Holton-Arms School in Maryland and the Miss Porter's School in Connecticut. She graduated from high school in 1947 and headed off to college.

Much like the education she received during her teenage years, Jackie's college career was unstable, and she moved around frequently, rarely staying at one college or university for much longer than a single year. Her college education began at Vassar College in Poughkeepsie, New York, which was then an all-girls school of great prestige. She spent two years there, the longest time she ever spent at a single institution. From there, Jackie had a defining experience, when she moved to France, where she studied first in Grenoble and later at the Sorbonne in Paris. French literature was her chosen major, which would assist her in both becoming fluent in French and later in her publishing work.

After returning from France, Jackie enrolled at George Washington University in Washington, D.C., receiving her bachelors of arts in French literature from the university in 1951. For the following summer, Jackie and her sister, who recently graduated from high school, travelled across Europe, a similar vacation to one taken three years earlier by 23 year old Bobby Kennedy after graduating from Harvard. Jackie would later write an account of the trip, *One Special Summer*, which would be her only autobiographical writing.

Chapter 3: World War II and the 1940s

John's Military Service and PT-109

In addition to having the benefit of seniority within the Kennedy family, the different ages of the brothers also meant that John had a much more active role in World War II than Bobby or Ted. By becoming decorated war heroes, both Joseph Jr. and John were establishing additional bona fides for future political office, although only John would survive the war to reap the reward.

Military service was a necessary component in John's political preparation, and John did have political ambitions of his own. When he enlisted in the military, however, his elder brother Joseph was still the family's prize and the one made of presidential material. Acutely aware of this, John tried to join the Army, but he was disqualified because of his health issues. He was, however, admitted to the Navy, due to family connections. His father's attaché in Great Britain was now a director in the Navy, and he ensured John received the position of ensign.

Like much of John's life, his service during the war is still a topic of controversy. John's time spent in the Navy was focused in the Pacific Theater of World War II, and by 1943, he was a commander of a patrol torpedo (PT) boat, number 109.

In August of 1943, John's boat, PT-109, was cut in half by a Japanese destroyer. In addition, boats 162 and 169 were also destroyed in the Solomon Islands. John survived the attack and famously saved nearly a dozen of his crew, one of whom he saved by swimming for several miles while clenching the crew member's lifejacket with his teeth. A member of the swim team at Harvard, he also did the bulk of the swimming when looking for food after the survivors reached a deserted island. For this, John received the Navy and Marine Corps Medal.

Ultimately, John and the survivors were rescued, but he had suffered a severe injury to his spine that would plague him for the rest of his life. He was sent to Boston to undergo surgery and recover. While in the hospital, he and his family learned that his elder brother Joseph had been killed in a bombing mission.

After recovering, John re-enlisted in the Navy and served on PT-59. He was honorably discharged in 1945, just before Japan's surrender and the end of the War. For his service, John received numerous military awards, among them a Purple Heart and a World War II Victory Metal. Though he was not yet President and perhaps only held that ambition in the back of his mind, he had already seen more combat than most Presidents.

John (far right) and the PT-109 crew

Bobby's Military Service and Marriage

Bobby joined the armed forces like his older brothers, but due to his age it came at the tail end of World War II, and he wasn't destined to have a military record like either of his older brothers. Bobby conducted naval training while a reservist and underwent training at Harvard University at Bates College in Lewiston, Maine. But despite his extensive training, Bobby's actual on-the-water military experience was quite limited. He was commissioned to serve beginning in February 1946 but was honorably discharged in May of that same year. His service had begun months after the war ended and just as the United States was dealing with post-war aftermath in Europe and Japan.

Bobby probably didn't mind the short service, because it allowed him to return to his studies at Harvard on a permanent basis, and as a smaller, thin young adult, he wasn't cut out for combat the same way his older brothers were. Thus, Bobby reenrolled at Harvard in 1946 with advanced standing, having received credit for his naval training as part of a V-12 program. At Harvard, Bobby was passionate in everything he did, both as a star football player and in the classroom, where he took great interest in politics, international affairs and the law.

After graduating from Harvard in 1948, Bobby embarked on a 6-month tour of Europe and the Middle East, which attests to the privileged nature his family's fortunes provided. During that trip, he witnessed the growing tensions between Muslims and Jews in Palestine, which he expected would boil over into a full-blown war. It was also the starting point in which he would begin to formulate his opinions on the issue that his assassin would later cite as the motive for murdering him.

After Harvard, Bobby decided law school was the path for him. That same year, he enrolled in law school at the University of Virginia. Bobby would graduate and go on to work legal jobs for nearly 15 years, but the most momentous event of his law school years was his marriage to Ethel Skakel.

As fate would have it, Ethel was close friends with Bobby's sister Jean, and ironically, Bobby met Ethel while he was dating Ethel's sister. When that relationship ended, Bobby and Ethel began their own relationship, bonding over a shared upbringing that was both privileged and devoutly Catholic. By 1946, the two of them were working together on John's Congressional campaign, and they were married in 1950.

Bobby and Ethel

Chapter 4: Climbing the Ladder, 1945-1960

Post-War Jobs

Fittingly, after World War II, the Kennedy brothers started following each other's footsteps. John's first non-military professional experience was in journalism, where he got his start after Joseph Sr. arranged for him to work with Hearst Chicago-Herald American, an international news service, in April of 1945. His first assignment was in San Francisco, where he covered the United Nations Conference, an historic moment that witnessed the formation of the modern United Nations.

John was a prolific writer, and newspaper mogul William Randolph Hearst was pleased with John's work. After his stint at the U.N., John was sent to London to cover the post-war British Parliamentary elections. John predicted that Winston Churchill and the Conservatives would lose the elections; the British people, Kennedy thought, were yearning for change. His prediction proved correct. The Labour Party swept the British elections that year, and the great Prime Minister Winston Churchill was removed from Downing Street.

William Randolph Hearst

John enjoyed his work with Hearst, and he was given numerous opportunities to learn about the effects of World War II on Europe, touring devastated German cities. He even had the opportunity to meet with Supreme Allied Commander, and future president, Dwight D. Eisenhower. Throughout his time abroad, John honed his foreign policy bona fides.

Like his brother John, Bobby began his career in journalism, not the law or politics. While John became a prolific writer under the tutelage of notorious newspaper magnate William Randolph Hearst, Bobby moved to San Francisco, where he covered the proceedings around the Peace Treaty with Japan.

In 1951, however, Kennedy decided to finally take up the law, joining the Criminal Division of the U.S. Department of Justice. Newly married and already with a newborn child, Bobby and his family moved to Washington, D.C., in the Georgetown neighborhood, for a brief period. A year later, he was transferred to the Eastern District in New York City.

Jackie spent the first of her post-college years the same way her future husband and brother-in-law did: in journalism. Jackie was first hired as a photographer for the *Washington Times-Herald,* where her position required her to surprise random people on the street with questions, and then take their photo as they responded. The pictures and answers would then run together in the paper, an entertaining kind of segment that remains a staple of newspapers today, and for this Jackie was dubbed the "Inquiring Photographer".

Representative John F. Kennedy

After less than a year with Hearst, Joseph Jr. began to prod John about his prospects for a career in politics. John returned to America in the fall of 1945, and his father gave him ample opportunities to give speeches throughout Massachusetts. Though they were generally well-received, Joseph Sr. had concerns that his son's more reserved and quiet style was not fitting of a politician. Unlike Ted or Bobby, John was generally shyer than the typical politician, often refusing to hobnob with voters after giving a speech.

Nonetheless, Joseph Sr. thought his son was suited for a more administrative sort of government job. He suggested John begin his career by running for Massachusetts Lieutenant Governor. Family friends and other Massachusetts politicos, however, were less certain. At just 28 years old, John would be strongly criticized for his lack of experience. The Lieutenant Governorship was a position that demanded expertise.

Besides, John had other ideas for himself. In 1946, the strongly Democratic 10th District House of Representatives seat in Massachusetts was vacated when its holder decided to run for Mayor of Boston. John thus seized the opportunity and ran for the seat. It was his first political campaign.

Like his other races, John's first political candidacy was ultimately successful, but not without enormous challenge. Opponents charged that he was a snob who could not relate to the working class constituents of the 10th District. Others said he had barely spent any time in the 10th since he was a child. It was a line of political attacks that each Kennedy would come to face.

Together with the Kennedy family, however, John countered these attacks effectively. His campaign lauded his position as a war hero. The Boston Catholic Church, perhaps prompted by Joseph's expensive contributions, loudly endorsed John for the seat. With the Kennedy fortune funding his campaign, John won the Democratic nomination and the election by rousing margins.

When Kennedy arrived in Congress in early 1947, he was surprised to find himself in the minority party. The 1946 elections had swept the Republicans into a majority that they hadn't held in over a decade. Regardless, John's initial participation in Congress gave the nation its first glimpse into his political positions. Unlike many post-New Deal Democrats (and both brothers), John was actually fairly conservative on fiscal issues. He opposed budget deficits and opposed tax cuts that would worsen deficits. Though many of his fellow Democrats drafted legislation supported by unions, John thought unions were ultimately self-interested in the same way corporations were; to John, they supported the interests of union leadership, not workers themselves. As a result, John's time in Congress reflected a mixed voting record. He was not a very partisan Democrat, and often voted with Republicans.

Ted Comes of Age

Although his grades were merely stellar, his attendance at Milton and family ties ensured that Ted followed his three older brothers to Harvard University, where he enrolled in September of 1950. Unlike his brothers, however, Ted matriculated at Harvard with an eye on athletics, not academics. While his siblings had been star students, Ted preferred football.

In keeping with his interests, Ted lived in the Winthrop House, an athlete-oriented dormitory on the Harvard campus. But because Ted was so keen on playing football, he knew he needed to maintain strong grades. To do so, however, he opted to cheat. He and his friends copied answers on a Spanish test in May 1951 and were caught. They were summarily expelled from school and told they could reapply in a year or two if they maintained good behavior over that time.

Having sidelined himself at Harvard, Ted needed something to do with his time, and for an athletic 19 year old, one good place for him in 1951 was Korea, where American forces had been fighting for several years and were on the verge of a stalemate. Kennedy enlisted in the US Army in 1951, for a term of four years, but Joseph Sr. used his political pull to ensure the duration of the term was for only two years. Kennedy trained at Fort Dix, and was shipped off to Europe, where he was stationed in Paris.

Paris was obviously a world away from Korea, and it wasn't exactly the front line during the Cold War either. At first glance, France seemed like a curious place for Ted to be deployed, but once again that was not his call. Having lost a son in World War II and watching John suffer a nearly permanent back injury, Joseph Sr. ensured that Ted would not see combat during the ongoing Korean War. If Ted had qualms about his cushy status, he didn't show it. By all accounts, he thoroughly enjoyed himself, traveling throughout Europe in his spare time and even climbing the Matterhorn in the Alps.

After two years with the Army, Ted successfully applied for readmission to Harvard and rejoined the school in 1953. This time, he worked on improving as a student. Naturally, at 6'2, 200 pounds, he also continued to play football, starring as an end on both offense and defense. By the time Ted graduated in 1956, he had caught the eye of the Green Bay Packers, who even contacted him. Ironically, Ted informed them that he was now planning to "go into another contact sport." Having seen John go from private citizenship to the halls of Congress so quickly, it was at least partially understandable why Ted would give up a potential athletic career to enter politics.

If Ted's decision to forgo football for politics wasn't evidence enough that he looked up to his brothers, his selection of a law school made it clear. Upon graduating from Harvard with a degree in History, Ted headed off to law school at the University of Virginia, which would seem like an odd choice for someone who lived in the Northeast most of his life but for the fact it was where Bobby had gone to law school.

However, Ted's time in law school, much like his years in Harvard, would come to be dominated by John's rising political career.

John Meets Jackie

Understandably, a beautiful, affluent and educated 22 year old caught the eye of many prospective bachelors during the early '50s, and it was also during this time that Jackie met a prospective husband, a stockbroker named John Husted Jr. The two met through the Social Register, which was a book that compiled the names and contact information of Americans from prominent families, located mainly in the Northeast. Because of her wealthy and prominent father, Jackie was listed in the book. Likewise, Husted was from a prominent family and was also listed in the book. As chance would have it, Husted's family counted Jackie's father and stepfather among their friends.

The two began dating, with Jackie commuting all the way to New York from Washington on weekends to be with Husted. The courtship was made easier by the fact that Jackie's father owned estates in and around the city, including one on East 74th Street that Jackie frequently stayed at while visiting Husted. By December 1951, the two were engaged to be married.

Ultimately, the marriage never took place. Jackie allegedly had second thoughts about Husted and considered him immature, while Husted came away from the engagement believing Jackie's mother thought him unsuitable. Her mother later said that Husted did not make enough money to support Jackie properly, even though he was doing quite well for a young man his age as a stockbroker. The engagement was called off in March 1952, and the two separated.

Ironically, Jackie met her future husband while engaged to her would-be husband. In 1951, both John and Jackie attended a party at the house of mutual friends, Charles and Martha Barlett. As the story goes, young Jackie caught Congressman Kennedy's eye, and he actually escorted her to her car in the hopes of leaving the party with her, only to find her fiancée, Husted, already in the car.

Only a few months after her engagement was broken off with Husted, Jackie was more formally introduced to the Massachusetts Congressman at another dinner party by their mutual friends. Due to their wealthy, Northeastern backgrounds, John and Jackie had long moved in the same social circles, with several mutual friends, some of whom introduced them in May 1952.

After that party, the two quickly began dating. John initially asked Jackie out but quickly withdrew the offer upon hearing that Jackie was engaged to another man. Jackie, however, clarified the situation: she had been engaged, but no longer was. She was free to go on a date with John and was, in fact, quite happy to. The couple hit things off, and about a year later, on June 25, 1953, the two were engaged. When the two met, John, who had served in the House of Representatives for about 5 years, was in the process of running for the U.S. Senate

Senator John Kennedy

John was reelected to the House twice and served there until 1952, but by then he had the presidency on his mind. Thus, he looked to climb the political ladder by deciding to run for a spot in the U.S. Senate, a better platform from which to gain national attention and run for President. Though the Senate had not typically produced many Presidents in recent years, it nonetheless seemed a viable option. John also considered the Governorship, but ultimately he thought the Senate suited him better, given his interest in international relations. The current Governor of Massachusetts, a Democrat, was considering running for the Senate as well. Kennedy waited for the Governor to make his decision before announcing his intent to run. When the Governor decided against the Senate, John opted in.

John's Republican opponent, Henry Cabot Lodge Jr., was running for reelection. Like him, the iconic Republican Senator was himself a war hero during World War II, and he was all the more noteworthy for being the first sitting Senator since the Civil War to serve in active duty. He was also from a prominent New England political family, perhaps one even more prominent than the Kennedy's. Predictably, both were Harvard alums.

Bobby resigned his position with the Department of Justice to free up time to assist his brother with his ultimately successful campaign. Having already earned a knack for successful campaigning in 1946, Bobby's nuts-and-bolts work in that campaign made him an ideal manager for his brother's 1952 Senate campaign. Ted, still just 20 years old, worked in a less prominent position in 1952.

Despite the stiff challenge, John prevailed by a narrow margin on Election Day, defeating Lodge 51.3 to 48.3%. His victory was due in large part to his appeal to "white ethnics," particularly Jews and Catholics throughout Massachusetts.

As a Senator, John's positions were relatively conservative. A major moment in his career came in 1957, when his procedural votes on Eisenhower's 1957 Civil Rights Act were seen as appeasements of Southern Democrats. He also made comments about the French War in Indochina, a precursor to the Vietnam War, and the French attempt to maintain its Algerian colony, which Senator Kennedy opposed. Senator Kennedy also refused to condemn Senator McCarthy's "red baiting," perhaps because McCarthy was a family friend. A final and controversial stance Senator Kennedy took was his position in favor of the St. Lawrence Seaway, a transportation system between Canada and the Great Lakes. The position was not favored in Massachusetts because many thought it would move economic productivity away from Massachusetts and send it westward towards upstate New York. His position received national attention as a courageous act, and partly inspired his later authoring of *Profiles in Courage*.

The Kennedy-Bouvier Wedding

   Given Kennedy's political ascent, and the combination of two wealthy Northeastern families, it isn't terribly surprising that the Kennedy-Bouvier wedding was one of the country's most important social events of the year. A sitting U.S. Senator – a young, handsome and rising star at that – was marrying the daughter of a wealthy stockbroker. The two families were of great notoriety in New England, and both owned mansions and family compounds throughout the Northeast, in such high-end locals as Newport, Cape Cod and the Hamptons.

   With over 1,300 people in attendance, the wedding was a grand affair. The marriage's reception followed at Hammersmith Farm in Newport, Rhode Island, which was a property owned by Jackie's family. Hammersmith was a Victorian Mansion that served as another summer home for Jackie during her childhood. The reception only added to the fairytale nature of the Kennedy wedding by offering a grand, sprawling estate along the New England seashore as the backdrop for celebration. Some of the memorabilia from the wedding, most notably Jackie's wedding dress, are still on display at the John F. Kennedy Library in Boston, and Hammersmith was open to tourists until the 1970s.

Hammersmith served as a summer retreat for the future First Family and was later sold for $8 million in 1999.

All was not perfect at the wedding, however. Notably, Jackie's own father, who had previously divorced her mother, was not able to attend to the wedding, or perform the traditional "handing over" of the daughter. His rampant alcoholism was cited as a cause of his absence.

After their wedding, the newly married couple headed off for Acapulco, Mexico, where they enjoyed their honeymoon. After a few weeks honeymooning, the couple returned to McLean, Virginia, where they were living while John served in the Senate.

John's Health and *Profiles in Courage*

Much like the description of the Kennedy presidency as "Camelot" belied the true nature of their troubled marriage, the fairytale nature of their wedding belied the fact that Jackie and John's early marriage was plagued by personal difficulties.

Despite his meteoric rise politically, John continued to suffer bad back issues as a result of his war wounds. He had been recovering from the back injury ever since, but he further complicated his injuries through games of football, probably an unwise idea given that his kid brother was a star end for Harvard, Since the war, his spine had deteriorated, to the point that he needed crutches to navigate the halls of the US Senate, and by 1954, John needed a potentially life-threatening surgery, which was performed at the Lahey Clinic. A metal plate was inserted into his spine to further prevent the deterioration of his lumbar vertebrae.

Though ultimately successful, the surgery nearly killed him. Within days of the operation, John developed a urinary tract infection, complicated by his Addison disease, which lessened his ability to fight infection. Antibiotics were not working, and John fell into a coma in late 1954. At one point, Joseph Sr. called in a priest to administer Catholic last rites.

In hindsight, doctors know that Kennedy's non-responsiveness to medication was due to his Addison's Disease, which complicated his ability to fight off disease and infection. At the time, however, little was known about Addison's Disease, and doctors did not consider its effects when operating on him.

Throughout the ordeal, Jackie was hysteric. Only married for less than two years, she thought her husband was going to die, leaving her a widow. The U.S. Senate was equally dismayed, fearing it would lose one of its most valued members. Within weeks, however, Kennedy came out of the coma and began to slowly recover. Though he was now conscious, his full recovery would occupy over a year and a half of his life, valuable time away from the U.S. Senate and the political limelight.

Eventually, John began to recover slowly. Jackie sensed her husband was depressed, fearing his personal health was holding back his professional and political advancement. She thus suggested he write a book about political courage. He took up her advice, and wound up authoring a Pulitzer-Prize winning book, *Profiles in Courage*. The book detailed the lives of historical American politicians who had to walk tight lines between personal convictions and constituent interests. Examples included John Quincy Adams, who defied popular opinion and political expediency in his fight against slavery. Although John won accolades for his book, it was widely suspected that it had actually been co-written by longtime speechwriter Ted Sorenson, who finally verified the rumor 45 years after his death.

The National Election of 1956

At the Democratic convention in 1956, John's name was thrown into the ring as an attractive Vice Presidential candidate. Putting Senator Kennedy on the ticket would help keep "white ethnics," who were tempted by Eisenhower, in the Democratic column. Additionally, he could deliver Massachusetts and other parts of the Northeast, which were considered "battleground" territories in the mid-1950's.

Ultimately, John didn't win the nomination, instead finishing in second. Delegates thought his Catholicism was still a liability, and his father privately believed the loss was a good thing because the chances of the incumbent Eisenhower losing were slim. Moreover, though he had won in Massachusetts with his local appeal, it was widely believed John was still too young for such a prominent position. As it turned out, the Democrats would lose the 1956 election to Eisenhower, while Kennedy had the good fortune of giving his name a national spotlight but not being associated with defeat.

John's Presidential ambitions were further hardened two years later, when he was reelected to the Senate by a landslide margin. The Republicans didn't even both to nominate an opponent. With no incumbent in the 1960 election, the Kennedys had laid the groundwork for a presidential run.

Bobby's Work in the Senate

Having resigned his position to successfully manage his brother's Senate campaign, Bobby was between jobs in late 1952, but his work in the Criminal Division of the U.S. Department of Justice investigating suspected Soviet agents made him an ideal assistant for another Senator whose political power was sharply rising. Through the backing and urging of his father, Bobby was appointed an assistant counsel of the U.S. Senate Permanent Subcommittee on Investigations by Senator Joseph McCarthy, who had established himself combating those he perceived to be Communists. Years before McCarthyism became political anathema and Senator McCarthy was censured and disgraced, Bobby grew to like the Senator and worked for nearly a year in that position.

In 1953, Bobby went to work on the Hoover Commission, which aimed to propose administrative changes in the federal government. In addition to being chaired by (and named after) former President Herbert Hoover, Bobby's father Joseph Sr. was part of the Commission. After that stint, Bobby served as the chief counsel for Senate Democrats over the next few years.

The highlight of Bobby's early career came when he served as an aide to Adlai Stevenson's 1956 Presidential Campaign. Though he had successfully managed his brother's Senate campaign in 1952, working in Stevenson's campaign allowed Bobby to learn the ins and outs of a Presidential campaign. Naturally, he was doing this in anticipation of his brother's own presidential campaign, which would come 4 years later. And ironically, despite learning much about politics and campaigning during the Election of 1956, Bobby was not fond of Stevenson as a politician, and actually voted for the Republican incumbent, Dwight Eisenhower.

Bobby spent the next few years serving as chief counsel in the Senate Labor Rackets Committee, a position he was well equipped for after he had battled teamsters in the Eastern District of New York. It was during this time that Bobby first crossed paths with infamous Teamsters leader Jimmy Hoffa, who he would very famously and openly grill during a televised hearing in the early '60s, earning him accolades for his dogged determination. After the assassination of President Kennedy, Hoffa famously remarked, "You know how the goddamn Kennedys have been hounding me, and you're asking me to honor the President's death." In 1964, Hoffa was convicted and jailed for corruption, famously disappearing in 1975, which remains one of the country's most mysterious murder cases. Though it is John's book, *Profiles in Courage*, which continues to be the best known book written by one of the Kennedys, Bobby published *The Enemy Within* in 1960, a comprehensively detailed look at the corruption within the Teamsters.

Still, Bobby was well aware that his work in the Senate Labor Rackets Committee was merely a prelude to the Election of 1960.

Ted's Life and Marriage in the '50s

With his name now catapulted onto a more national level, John ran for reelection in 1958, and again it was a family effort. This time, it was Ted's turn to run his brother's campaign, becoming the official chairman of the 1958 reelection campaign. John's large margin of victory in the 1958 reelection had many speculating that he would seek the Presidency in 1960.

Still just 26 years old in 1958, Ted had chaired a U.S. Senate campaign before he finished law school. 1958 was monumental for other reasons too. Ted graduated from the University of Virginia School of Law in 1959, but not before he met Virginia Joan Bennett. Bennett was a former model who attended Manhattanville College in New York. In October 1957, Ted gave a speech to dedicate a gymnasium at Manhattanville in honor of his sister Kathleen, who had been killed nearly a decade earlier in a plane crash. While there, sister Jean introduced Ted and Joan, and the two quickly began dating. Within months, the two were engaged to be married, and they wedded about a year after meeting, on November 29th, 1958, in Bronxville, New York.

Initially, their marriage was a happy one. The couple enjoyed their life in and around New York, and Ted's law career was just beginning, having passed the Massachusetts Bar in 1959 after graduating from Virginia. Over the course of their marriage, the couple had 3 children: Kara, Edward Jr., and Patrick.

Ted and Joan

Joan was marrying Ted at an awfully busy time for the Kennedy family, and politics quickly came to dominate the marriage. By 1959, John was sure he would seek the Presidency in 1960, and with that, the entire Kennedy family was drawn into the campaign, including Ted, who had performed an exemplary campaign just a year earlier.

The Kennedy Families Grow

The First Family in 1962

After his recovery from back surgery, John and Jackie began expanding the family dynasty with children, but as with the earlier ordeal the couple had just experienced, the path to children was not easy.

In 1955, the year after John's surgery, Jackie suffered a miscarriage. Their next attempt resulted in an even worse tragedy, when Jackie gave birth to a stillborn girl on August 23rd, 1956. This first Kennedy would eventually be buried alongside her parents at Arlington.

Thankfully, Jackie's next pregnancy was successful, and on November 27, 1957, daughter Caroline Bouvier Kennedy was born at the Cornell Medical Center in New York City. Jackie named the daughter after her own sister, Caroline Lee Bouvier, and her grandmother, Caroline Ewing Bouvier. Like her mother, Caroline quickly developed an interest in equestrian and horse riding. This would be a defining part of her personality in the White House, where the first surviving Kennedy daughter would spend most of her most formative years.

Meanwhile, Bobby's family grew so large so fast that he eventually bought a spacious house and sprawling estate, known as Hickory Hill, from his older brother John in the 1950s. Along with the 12 children Bobby and Ethel had from 1951-1968, Hickory Hill housed a zoo for son Robert Jr., with inhabitants like seals and even an elephant. While Bobby pursued his political career, Ethel raised the children and capably served the role of host, holding parties and gatherings that included guests as varied as historian Arthur Schlesinger, actress Judy Garland, and Beatles legend John Lennon. Jackie considered her brother-in-law's household so rowdy and rambunctious that she would not let her own kids visit it.

Chapter 5: The Election of 1960

Deciding to Run for President and Winning the Democratic Nomination

Privately, John and his father Joe had discussed the 1960 Presidential Election since Kennedy's Vice-Presidential hopes in 1956. John thought his Catholicism was the biggest barrier to the Presidency, while his father thought otherwise. To Joseph Sr., the nation had grown beyond its anti-Catholic sentiments and was ready to accept a Catholic President. Furthermore, since the 1956 Convention, the media had viewed Senator Kennedy as the frontrunner for the Democratic nomination. Polls of Democratic voters confirmed this view, showing Senator Kennedy in a tie with former nominee Adlai Stevenson for the 1960 nomination.

In late 1959, John announced his candidacy for the Presidency of the United States. Members of the Democratic Party elite, however, held reservations. Coming off the popular Eisenhower Presidency, the Democrats felt they had no room to nominate a "risky" candidate. Many still saw John's youth and his Catholicism as liabilities that could give the election to the Republicans in a close race. President Eisenhower's Vice-President, Richard Nixon, was favored to win the Republican nomination. Having successfully rehabilitated his image with the infamous "Checkers Speech", the experienced Nixon seemed a formidable candidate against the youthful and seemingly inexperienced Kennedy.

Richard Nixon

Other members of the Democratic elite stirred factions of the party against Kennedy. Among the most important anti-Kennedy leaders was Eleanor Roosevelt, who despised Joseph Sr. and thought his son to be too conservative. In part because of Mrs. Roosevelt, liberal Democrats were increasingly deterred from the Kennedy candidacy.

At the start of the campaigning, a poll of Congressional Democrats put John in fourth behind Lyndon Johnson, Adlai Stevenson and Stuart Symington for the nomination. Stevenson had long been a national figure, and Lyndon Johnson was one of the most influential members in Congress. Kennedy thus had a difficult campaign on his hands. Winning the nomination would require convincing Democratic liberals of his candidacy (despite his fairly conservative Congressional voting record), ensuring his religion would not be a distraction or a negative, and beating several potentially tough opponents.

Ultimately, the political environment proved ideal for Senator Kennedy to run for president. Throughout the few primaries that were conducted that year, John had the opportunity to prove his broad appeal to the Convention's party elders. His win in the largely white and Protestant state of West Virginia seemed to clinch his claim that he did not just appeal narrowly to fellow Catholics. At the Democratic Convention in Los Angeles, Kennedy won the nomination on the first ballot.

The Kennedy Campaign: A Family Affair

John F. Kennedy's campaign in 1960 was historic for several reasons, one of them being the extent to which it was a family affair involving all of the Kennedys. Bobby informally led the Kennedy for President Campaign of 1960, an historic campaign for many reasons. The extent to which the candidate's entire family was involved in John's presidential campaign was unprecedented, but the Kennedys were uniquely geared to produce a President, and all available manpower from the family worked on the effort. In addition to managing the campaign, Bobby proved an effective ideological counterweight to his more conservative brother. When Dr. Martin Luther King was arrested during the campaign, John called his wife, Coretta Scott King, at Bobby's urging.

While Bobby informally managed the campaign, Ted was charged with leading the campaign in the Western States. Ted's campaigning was especially critical during the 1960 Democratic primaries, which at the time required corralling delegates to support Kennedy at the National Convention. Though there were some open voting primaries, this practice was not widely used until later elections. Ted supported his brother at critical junctures, securing votes for Kennedy from states like Wisconsin, Wyoming and Colorado. With the strongman Texan Senator Lyndon B. Johnson also running in the primaries, Ted's task was a difficult one. He had been tasked with trying to convince Westerners to support a New Englander over a native son.

Jackie was initially enthused about the campaign. When she married John years earlier, she married a Representative-turned-Senator and was well aware of John's growing political ambitions. She married into the Kennedy family fully expecting politics and campaigns to be a dominant part of her married life. Moreover, Jackie was well-equipped for campaigning in an era where television and the media were becoming a more prominent part of American life. Her beauty was an obvious asset to the Kennedy campaign.

In early 1960, however, Jackie's intention to enthusiastically campaign was halted when she learned she was pregnant for the fourth time. Because of her earlier miscarriage, doctors advised that she stay at home and not campaign too eagerly. Jackie took this advice, and decided to campaign only occasionally, though she spent much of her time returning letters and phone calls regarding the campaign from the family's Georgetown apartment. She also wrote a column in national newspapers called the "Campaign Wife."

As a glamorous and beautiful young woman, Jackie had enormous appeal on the campaign. At age 31, Kennedy's victory would make her one of the youngest First Ladies in history. Additionally, her aristocratic background, worldliness and knowledge of multiple languages, particularly French, made her an overnight star. She represented a stark difference to her would-be First Lady counterpart, Pat Nixon, who could not come close to becoming the media darling Jackie did. Of course, Jackie's husband enjoyed the same advantage over opponent Richard Nixon.

Picking a Running Mate

Perhaps Bobby's biggest contribution to the Kennedy campaign was his involvement with the decision concerning a running mate. John preferred Senate Majority Leader Lyndon B. Johnson of Texas for a variety of reasons. Electorally, he thought Johnson made sense: being from Texas, he could help balance Kennedy's decidedly New England-centric appeal. Additionally, Johnson was much older than the youthful Kennedy, which would help deflect concerns about the candidate's age and inexperience. And in the realm of governing, Johnson was a veteran in Washington, having risen to the position of Senate Majority Leader and becoming one of the most powerful wielders of power in the history of that body. Johnson's experience would prove critical in governing the nation, as he had the connections and know-how that John Kennedy admittedly did not.

Bobby, however, was not convinced that Johnson was a good selection. Candidly, Bobby thought Lyndon Johnson was an intellectual lightweight, an accusation tinged with sectionalist prejudices. Bobby, from Massachusetts, thought the Texas Senator was wholly unintelligent. When John called Johnson to ask him to be the Vice Presidential nominee, Bobby reportedly contacted Johnson to ask that he decline the offer. This accusation has never been confirmed; however, it is known that Johnson contacted John again to confirm that he had actually been offered the nomination.

Regardless of what actually occurred, the damage between Bobby and Johnson had been done. Though the personal relationship between the Texas Senator and John was not strained, any semblance of friendship between Bobby and Johnson was over. While this may not have seemed relatively important at the time, when nobody could foresee Vice President Johnson succeeding President Kennedy, the relationship between LBJ and Bobby would play a prominent role in the Election of 1968.

The General Election

In the general election, Kennedy and Johnson faced Vice President Richard Nixon and Former Senator Henry Cabot Lodge, who John had defeated for the Senate seat in Massachusetts 8 years earlier. To open the campaign, Kennedy gave his famous New Frontier Speech at the Democratic Convention. In it, he branded his forward-looking ambitions for the United States.

Nevertheless, the 1960 election focused heavily on John's Roman Catholic religion. Though Bobby was always the most devout in the family, John had become only the second Catholic nominated for President, after Al Smith in 1928. Groups for religious freedom contended that Kennedy's Catholicism would make governing the nation as President difficult. Many were suspicious that he would accept demands from the Pope and the Catholic Hierarchy. By September, Kennedy closed the issue in a speech in Houston, where he said he was running to be a "President who happens to be Catholic," not a "Catholic President." For the remainder of the campaign, Kennedy's religion no longer fascinated the media, though it was likely still privately on the minds of many voters.

Undoubtedly the most important moment in the 1960 campaign came when Kennedy and Nixon faced off in the first-ever televised Presidential debate. On September 26, 1960, a little over a month until Election Day, the two candidates met in Chicago for a CBS-sponsored debate. Though Nixon went into the debate favored to win, by the end of the night it was clear that Nixon had yet to understand or master the importance of television. 70 million tuned in, while millions more listened on radio. Those who only heard the debate on radio believed Nixon had won the contest, but those watching saw a pale, sickly looking older man standing next to a young, tan man who looked invigorated. Americans trusted their eyes instead of their ears, and the debate turned a slight Nixon lead in the polls into a slight Kennedy lead.

After the debate, John spent the remaining month of the campaign patching together a viable Election Day coalition. African-Americans were an important piece of the Democratic coalition, but Kennedy's past hesitance on civil rights issues put that voting bloc in jeopardy. He decided to risk losing Southern white segregationists, and opted to come out more loudly in support of civil rights. This eventually won him the endorsement of Martin Luther King Jr.

By November, the gap between the two candidates was paper thin. Kennedy remained strong among "white ethnics," labor and African-Americans, while Nixon appealed to rural Protestants, the West Coast, and parts of the South. On Election Day, the popular vote was as close as polls suggested: Kennedy won by a hair, with 49.7% to Nixon's 49.5%. The Electoral College vote, however, was a different story, with Kennedy winning with 303 votes to Nixon's 219. The vote was so close that many still accuse Kennedy and his surrogates of fixing the election, with charges of fraud clouding matters in Texas and Illinois. Nixon would later be praised for refusing to contest the election, but in the following decades it was made clear how much his surrogates had tried to overturn the election.

Regardless, John F. Kennedy had just become the youngest man ever elected President, and the first Roman Catholic. He was sworn in as the 35th President of the United States on January 20, 1961. Despite heavy snow, the festivities surrounding Kennedy's inauguration were exciting. President Kennedy attended Mass at the Holy Trinity Catholic Church in Georgetown, a gesture that greatly pleased his fellow Catholic Americans, who were thrilled to have a President "of their own." And of course, most famously, in his inaugural address he asked Americans to "ask not what your country can do for you, but ask what you can do for your country."

The Kennedy family's dream of a President Kennedy had finally come true.

Chapter 6: Camelot, 1960-1963

A New First Family

In many ways, John F. Kennedy and his young family were the perfect embodiment of the '60s. The decade began with a sense of idealism, personified by the attractive Kennedy, his beautiful and fashionable wife Jackie, and his young children. Months into his presidency, Kennedy exhorted the country to reach for the stars, calling upon the nation to send a man to the Moon and back by the end of the decade. In 1961, Kennedy made it seem like anything was possible, and Americans were eager to believe him. The Kennedy years were fondly and famously labeled "Camelot," by Jackie herself, suggesting an almost mythical quality about the young President and his family.

As if the youth of the Kennedys wasn't obvious enough during the Fall of 1960, the point was driven home in the weeks after the Election when Jackie made history by becoming the only First Lady-elect to give birth. On November 25, 1960, less than two months before her husband's inauguration, Jackie gave birth to her second child and first son, who was named after his father. Just as she had with Caroline, Jackie gave birth to John through Caesarian section. John was delivered at the Georgetown University Hospital just 16 days after his father's election to the Presidency.

Jackie's ascension to the First Ladyship was thus very different from her predecessors. Unlike previous First Ladies, who occupied the intervening months between election and inauguration by preparing to move to the White House, Jackie focused on her children. With a newborn infant son, Jackie had no time to prepare for life on Pennsylvania Avenue.

To make up for her inability to tend to traditional First Lady duties, Jackie made an unprecedented move and hired a personal social secretary, Letitia Baldridge. Baldridge served as a press and media secretary, crafting Jackie's public image for the media. Presidents before had had press secretaries, but no First Lady ever had.

Baldridge helped uphold and strengthen Jackie's image as a fabulous, beautiful and socially astute woman. She ensured that Jackie was aware of social matters and always had the most beautiful clothes and accessories when appearing in public. With Baldridge's help, Jackie was able to more appropriately balance her obligations to the White House with those to her young children.

Promotions for the Family

Despite the allure of John's victory in 1960, President Kennedy still had to govern in the real world, which was far less interested in a mystical narrative. From the beginning, Kennedy's young presidency had to manage some self-inflicted injuries. The first would involve the Kennedy family.

Given how close Bobby and John were, and the important role Bobby had played in the 1960 election (not to mention the previous elections), it is not surprising that the new President would tap his younger brother for some sort of position in his administration. After all, Bobby was a veteran insider in the U.S. Senate for the better part of the '50s, without being an elected Senator. But the public was not prepared for just how high John would appoint Bobby.

Upon becoming the President-Elect, John made an unprecedented move and appointed his own brother to be the Attorney General of the United States. Though Bobby wanted the job, he was very worried that the appointment would saddle the Kennedy Administration with an unnecessary controversy. His prediction quickly proved correct. While President Kennedy joked that he " can't see that it's wrong to give him a little legal experience before he goes out to practice law", the public and media found it far less funny. In addition to looking like blatant nepotism, the appointment of the President's brother to a Cabinet post made the Kennedys seem like the royalty that many accused them of being. Additionally, Bobby was not the most qualified Attorney General; the President's quip aside, Bobby did not exactly have a long and prosperous legal career behind him.

Regardless, though, John wanted Bobby at his side, valuing both his abilities and as a confidant. The two brothers had become particularly close throughout the Presidential campaign, and John admired his brother's advice. The President took his argument to the public, saying that there was precedent for seeing the Attorney General as a loyal advisor to the President, and that he had the right to choose someone who he was personally close to. The Attorney General, above all Cabinet posts, was the one most loyal to the President and the one that took orders and commands most directly from the President himself. With that logic, the choice of Bobby was justified. Besides, the Kennedys anticipated that the Attorney General would devote resources to combating the Teamsters and union connections with the mob, a battle that Bobby had much experience in already.

Shortly after President Kennedy was sworn in, Bobby was put up for nomination hearings before the United States Senate. After performing well, he was sworn in to head the Justice Department in Washington.

On top of that nomination controversy, there was another brother the Kennedy family hoped to take care of. Having been elected President, John naturally had to resign his Senate seat, and as a young adult who had witnessed and participated in his brother's successful political campaigns, Ted was now eager for his own political career and wanted to run for the Senate seat. After family discussions, it was decided by Joseph Sr. that Ted should run for Senate in 1962, over the objections of John and Bobby. Thus, at the new president's request, the Governor of Massachusetts appointed an old Kennedy family friend who would not seek reelection to the Senate in 1962, meaning there would be no incumbent in 1962.

With John's former Senate due to be open, many naturally turned to the only Kennedy viable to take the seat. Even in 1960, people had been circulating Ted's name as a possible replacement, not realizing Ted wasn't even eligible yet. At 28, Ted was still so young that he didn't meet the Senate's age requirement.

Cuba and the Bay of Pigs

Within just a month of becoming President, the issue of communist Cuba became central to the Kennedy Presidency. On February 3rd, 1961, President Kennedy called for a plan to support Cuban refugees in the U.S. A month later, John created the Peace Corps, a program that trained young American volunteers to help with economic and community development in poor countries. Both programs were integral pieces of the Cold War: each was an attempt to align disadvantaged groups abroad with the United State and the West, against the Soviet Union and its Communist satellites.

Cuba and the Cold War boiled over in April, when the Kennedy Administration moved beyond soft measures to direct action. From April 17-20, 1,400 CIA-trained Cuban exiles landed on the beaches of Western Cuba in an attempt to overthrow Fidel Castro. This plan, which Kennedy called the "Bay of Pigs," had been originally drafted by the Eisenhower Administration. The exiles landed in Cuba and were expected to be greeted by anti-Castro forces within the country. After this, the US was to provide air reinforcement to the rebels, and the Castro regime would slowly be overthrown.

By April 19th, however, it became increasingly clear to Kennedy that the invasion would not work. The exiles were not, as expected, greeted by anti-Castro forces. Instead, the Cuban government captured or killed all of the invaders. No U.S. air reinforcement was ever provided, flummoxing both the exiles and American military commanders. The Bay of Pigs had been an unmitigated disaster.

On April 21st, in a White House press conference, President Kennedy accepted full responsibility for the failure, which had irreparably damaged Cuban-American relations. From then on, Fidel Castro remained wary of a U.S. invasion, which would have serious implications when the USSR began planning to move missiles into Cuba, precipitating another crisis a year and a half later. Between April and the following year, the U.S. and Cuba negotiated the release of the imprisoned exiles, who were finally released in December of 1962, in exchange for $55.5 million dollars worth of food and medicine.

Just months into his Presidency, Kennedy was severely embarrassed. Hailed as a foreign policy expert with heroic military experience during the campaign, Kennedy's ability to conduct American foreign policy was now firmly in question, and it was eagerly put to the test by the Soviet Prime Minister, Nikita Khrushchev. When the two leaders negotiated in June 1961 at Vienna, Kennedy later told his brother Bobby that it was "like dealing with Dad. All give and no take."

Khrushchev and Kennedy meet at Vienna

The Space Race Begins

In 1957, at a time when people were concerned about communism and nuclear war, many Americans were dismayed by news that the Soviet Union was successfully launching satellites into orbit. Among these concerned Americans was President Eisenhower, whose space program was clearly lagging a few years behind the Soviets' space program. In 1957, the Soviets successfully launched Laika the dog into orbit, while NASA just seemed to be dogging it. Americans who could view Soviet rockets in the sky were justifiably worried that Soviet satellites in orbit could soon be spying on them, or, even worse, dropping nuclear bombs on them.

April 1961 was certainly a bad month for President Kennedy's Cold War bona fides. Even before the Bay of Pigs, America's Cold War prospects seemed even bleaker when the Soviet Union launched Yuri Gagarin into space, making him the first human to travel outside of earth. It was an enormous scientific and technologic feat, and it showcased the industriousness of the USSR. The Cold War was not merely a contest over economic and military power; it was also a battle for prestige. On this final point, the Soviet Union's entry into space gave it an enormous lead.

In response, President Kennedy spoke to a joint session of Congress in May, in which he proposed one-upping the Soviets by not only sending a man to space, but by sending a man to the moon. On May 25, 1961, President Kennedy asked the nation to "commit itself to achieving the goal, before this decade is out, of landing a man on the Moon and returning him safely to the Earth." While Kennedy is still hailed today for his push to land a man on the moon within a decade, Eisenhower's administration had already been designing plans for the Apollo space program by 1960, a year before Soviet cosmonaut Yuri Gagarin orbited the Earth and two years before John Glenn became the first American to orbit the Earth.

President Kennedy's commitment to space initiatives prior to Yuri Gagarin's mission was mixed, however. As a Senator, he had opposed the Eisenhower Administration's research funding to space exploration. As President, he changed his position in response to the Soviet Union's advances.

Though Kennedy was not alive to witness the U.S. achieve this mission, his rally cry was on everyone's mind when Apollo 11 fulfilled his vision on July 20, 1969, landing on the Moon.

Jackie Renovates the White House

Renovating the White House

Jackie giving the famous televised White House tour in February 1962

Historically, First Ladies have carved out a niche of their own during their husbands' presidencies. Some remained behind the scenes, while others like Hillary Clinton and Nancy Reagan spearheaded certain policy initiatives for their husbands' administrations. As the mother of two young children, Jackie was positioned to play a unique role as a First Lady, and when she entered the White House, she realized the importance of juggling media interest in the First Family with the privacy necessary to raise her young children normally. Jackie did so by emphasizing that her personal priorities rested with her children first, politics second.

Still, Jackie was well aware of her role in the narrative of the Kennedy presidency, and she gave Americans and the press just enough glimpses of life inside the White House to keep them wanting more. While raising Caroline and John Jr., Jackie made time to greatly renovate the White House. With an avid interest in history, the arts, and aesthetics in general, Jackie was eager to reinvigorate the historic nature of the White House. Even before Inauguration Day, she was drafting plans to conduct historic preservation projects on the building and to redecorate the more private quarters of the building, which would make them more suitable for young children living there.

As First Lady, Jackie created the White House Historical Association, which aimed to preserve and protect the historic nature of the nation's Executive Mansion. She wrote a book called *The White House: An Historic Guide*, and through the Historical Association, she was able to raise the needed funds to restore the building. She worked with Congress to pass laws to help protect the building, which included the creation of the position of White House Curator, a permanent federal job. Furthermore, she ensured that the furniture inside the White House would remain the property of the federal government through the Smithsonian Institute. Previously, Presidents had simply taken furniture with them as they left the White House, which Jackie thought made the White House an unfortunate and unappreciated national landmark.

Within the White House, Jackie utilized the expertise of furniture collector Henry du Pont and designer Sister Parish to remodel and redecorate the building. Among her projects around the White House included the redecorating of the Blue Room to coincide with the architectural era of the Second Empire style, harkening all the way back to the presidency of James Madison. She also made headway on the White House lawns, replanting and refurbishing the Rose Garden.

Even outside the immediate White House grounds, Jackie fought for historic preservation. In the Lafayette Park across the street, Jackie lobbied to make sure the historic park was not destroyed, which was the intention at the time. She hoped it would remain as it was, and that the historic buildings on site were maintained.

The Blue Room in 1962

Jackie's efforts culminated with her iconic guided tour of the White House in February 1962, televised by CBS. Explaining the renovations, Jackie led Americans into a place not only served as base of power but as the home for a family of four, telling viewers, "I just feel that everything in the White House should be the best -- the entertainment that's given here. If it's an American company you can help, I like to do that. If not -- just as long as it's the best."

Jackie's tour of the White House was so widely praised that the video of the tour was distributed across the world to over 100 nations. Two months later, a special Academy of Television Arts and Sciences Trustees Award was awarded to Jackie for that televised tour. Ironically, the woman who was so adept at cultivating public opinion and positive press was too camera-shy to accept the award, having Lady Bird Johnson, Vice President Johnson's wife, accept it for her.

Visiting an Art Gallery in Washington D.C., March 1961

Jackie was also a longtime patron of the arts, and hoped to use the White House to showcase the power of American artists. She vocally supported the creation of a National Arts Center in Washington. Working off a French model, she thought a nation's capitol should be used to showcase its artistic prowess.

Since the National Arts Center was moving along slowly, Jackie decided to use the White House to host artists. She hosted performances of Shakespeare, jazz and other fine arts right on Pennsylvania Avenue, all of which were performed by American artists and actors in the hopes of demonstrating America's artistic culture.

Among Jackie's other artistic accomplishments was the securing of the loan of the Mona Lisa from France's famed Louvre Museum. The Mona Lisa was (and is) among the most famous pieces of art in the world, and putting it on loan to the U.S. said volumes about France's respect for American art.

Jackie left a legacy of the arts that endures to this day. She lobbied heavily for the creation of the National Endowments of the Arts and Humanities, which continue to fund arts and humanities projects within the country today. She modeled many of her government projects on departments created in France, a nation she clearly adored.

Civil Rights
Of all the Kennedys, Bobby is remembered as the most ideological, and nowhere was this clearer than on the issue of Civil Rights. While John was a more cautious and conservative mover, Bobby dove headfirst into Civil Rights issues across the south. Though he is still remembered notoriously for ordering the wiretapping of Martin Luther King after FBI Director J. Edgar Hoover informed him that some of King's associates had suspected Communist ties, Bobby came to be seen as a very vigilant and public supporter of equality across the South, and

he championed desegregation within the federal government itself, once taking Vice President Johnson to task for maintaining an all-white staff.

By May 1962, when asked what issue posed the greatest problem ahead for his office, Bobby answered, "Civil Rights."

Bobby and Martin Luther King Jr.

Less than a month after the failed Bay of Pigs Invasion, Bobby's attention was turned to a matter that directly involved the Attorney General's Office. After a 1960 Supreme Court decision in *Boynton v. Virginia*, bus segregation was made illegal on new grounds: it violated the interstate commerce clause of the Constitution, by regulating the movement of people across state lines.

With this victory in hand, the Freedom Rides of 1961 began. Organized primarily by a new group – the Congress on Racial Equality (CORE) – the Freedom Rides followed the same guidance that fueled the success of other boycotts – nonviolent direct action. The purpose of the Freedom Rides was to test the Supreme Court's decision by riding from Virginia to Louisiana on integrated buses. It would also notably become the first major Civil Rights event that included a large segment of white participants.

Beginning in the summer of 1961, the Freedom Riders began their trips. They consisted of people from across the United States, of all races and backgrounds. The point of their mission was to show that peaceful integration aboard busses was possible. Peace was not to come, however. While the protesters themselves were peaceful, they were greeted with attacks when their buses entered the South. Particularly in Birmingham and Montgomery, Alabama, and throughout Mississippi, bus riders were greeted by mobs of whites, many of them affiliated with both the Ku Klux Klan and even local police forces. White activists, who were viewed by the Ku Klux Klan as betraying their race, took the worst beatings of all, and no one with power in the South was willing to enforce Federal laws allowing desegregation aboard interstate buses.

Attorney General Kennedy was dismayed by the violence, which he saw as both illegal, immoral, and as an international embarrassment. How could the United States support freedom abroad when its citizens at home were not free to ride busses? Although King would later thank him for having the federal government use force that summer, Bobby's intervention has gone down as somewhat controversial. Rather than unequivocally supporting the constitutional rights of the Freedom Riders, he instead struck a deal with governors across the South, whereby the governors agreed to protect the physical safety of the riders from mob violence but were still allowed to arrest Freedom Riders for violating segregation rules. Bobby thought this was the legally sound decision; the Riders were not entitled to violate segregation laws, which were still technically legal in the South, but their right to peaceful protest should also be protected.

This decision struck many as a weak and uninspiring compromise. Bobby, however, later ordered the Interstate Commerce Committee to officially enforce its decision to make interstate bus segregation illegal. The ICC complied, which allowed an institution with tangible authority to enforce bus desegregation. At the time, no agency with real authority was willing to enforce the law: Southern law enforcement agents were certainly not willing to allow desegregation. While this move was not publicly lauded, privately it did much to support the cause of the Freedom Riders.

Another major Civil Rights battle erupted in 1962, when James Meredith, an African-American, attempted to enroll at the University of Mississippi but was denied on the basis of being black. The James Meredith case represented another incident where a Southern state completely ignored the orders of a federal court, which fundamentally defied the principles and basis of American law and order. Earlier, a federal court had ordered the University of Mississippi to admit James Meredith to the University, and the state of Mississippi was required by law to enforce the action.

The Governor of Mississippi, Ross Barnett, personally opposed Meredith's enrollment at the University. He had the legislature pass an act barring anyone convicted of a crime from enrolling at the University. With this, Barnett claimed to have the "legal authority" to ban Meredith, because Meredith had been convicted of illegal voter registration, after having registered to vote without passing the proper tests required in the state. Those tests, however, were notoriously prejudiced against African-Americans, and effectively barred all blacks from voting.

Having come after the *Brown v. Board of Education* decision made segregation in schools illegal, Attorney General Kennedy thought the move required decisive action. Kennedy thus became personally involved in negotiations with Governor Barnett, threatening to arrest the governor and send in federal troops to enforce federal law within the state. Barnett yielded, allowing Meredith to enroll, but a white mob predictably attacked Meredith, prompting the Attorney General to send in federal U.S. Marshals to protect Meredith. To reinforce his brother's actions, President Kennedy also sent in a division of the U.S. Army to enforce law and order at the University of Mississippi.

The federal government sentenced Governor Barnett to a term in jail and a $10,000 fine for contempt of federal law. After ensuring Meredith's attendance in 1962, a similar situation broke out in 1963, when Alabama's Governor George Wallace personally prevented two African-American students from enrolling in the University of Alabama. Again, the Kennedy Administration sent in federal troops against the state's Governor. Attorney General Kennedy had, at last, taken a decisive and authoritative stance on the Civil Rights Movement in the South, coming out in favor of African-Americans against the Ku Klux Klan and the white establishment in the region.

During his presidency, President Kennedy proposed a limited civil rights act that focused primarily on voting rights, but it avoided more controversial topics like equal employment and desegregation. Kennedy, of course, had an eye on reelection, aiming to toe the line between maintaining political support in the South while also holding liberal Democrats. Nevertheless, his administration never gained any traction on a Civil Rights bill, with a coalition of Southern Democrats and Republicans preventing any action on one.

Vietnam

At the end of Kennedy's first year in office, the U.S. sent its first direct military support to South Vietnam, with two Army Helicopters arriving to the country on December 11th, 1961. This move was part of a long-standing commitment, begun by the Eisenhower Administration, to prevent the spread of communism into Southeast Asia. Furthermore, South Vietnam was one of the Southeast Asian countries that the United States vowed to help defend during negotiations over the armistice that ended the Korean War. President Kennedy was initially reluctant to devote a full-scale military presence to the country, but his position was continually evolving throughout his Presidency.

President Kennedy also felt that the South Vietnamese themselves did not want an American presence in their country. By 1963, this was increasingly apparent to the president, but, on the other hand, he felt the Southeast Asian territory was critical to preventing the spread of communism. This concept was fueled largely by the "Domino Theory" that had dominated Cold War foreign policy thinking. John also worried that giving up on Vietnam would further weaken his foreign policy credentials and chances at reelection in 1964.

Throughout 1962 and 1963, President Kennedy's primary interest in Vietnam was to better understand how much the South Vietnamese wanted or did not want an American presence. He sent numerous ambassadors, among them his former opponent Henry Cabot Lodge Jr., to the country to investigate. Kennedy, however, was frustrated when multiple investigations returned widely different accounts. The issue remained unresolved until President Johnson took over the policy and dramatically increased the American military presence in the middle of the decade.

Cuban Missile Crisis

The issue of communist Cuba came to a head in a big way in October of 1962. With the help of spy planes, U.S. intelligence discovered the Soviets were building nuclear missile sites in Cuba. The president officially learned of this on October 16th.

It went without saying that nuclear missile sites located just miles off the coast of the American mainland posed a grave threat to the country, especially because missiles launched from Cuba would reach their targets in mere minutes. That would throw off important military balances in nuclear arms and locations that had previously (and subsequently) ensured the Cold War stayed cold. Almost all senior American political figures agreed that the sites were offensive and needed to be removed, but how? Members of the U.S. Air Force wanted to take out the sites with bombing missions and launch a full-scale invasion of Cuba, but Kennedy, however, was afraid that such an action could ignite a full-scale escalation leading to nuclear war.

Here again, Bobby served as a critical advisor to the President and a counterweight to the aggressive posturing of military brass. Though he had previously taken aggressive stances in Cuba, Bobby was one of the voices who opposed outright war and helped craft the eventual plan: a blockade of Cuba. That was the decision John ultimately reached as well, deciding on a naval blockade of all Soviet ships to be the better option.

On October 22, 1962, President Kennedy addressed the nation to inform them of the crisis. He told Americans that the "purpose of these bases can be none other than to provide a nuclear strike capability against the Western Hemisphere." Speaking of the threat to the nuclear weapon balance maintained in previous years, Kennedy stated, "For many years, both the Soviet Union and the United States, recognizing this fact, have deployed strategic nuclear weapons with great care, never upsetting the precarious status quo which insured that these weapons would not be used in the absence of some vital challenge." Thus, Kennedy announced a blockade, warning, "To halt this offensive buildup a strict quarantine on all offensive military equipment under shipment to Cuba is being initiated. All ships of any kind bound for Cuba from whatever nation or port will, if found to contain cargoes of offensive weapons, be turned back."

Beginning on October 24th, the US began inspecting all Soviet ships traveling in the Caribbean. Any ships carrying missile parts would not be allowed to enter Cuba. Additionally, President Kennedy demanded that the Soviets remove all nuclear missile sites from Cuba. In response, Soviet premier Khrushchev called the blockade "an act of aggression propelling humankind into the abyss of a world nuclear-missile war".

Kennedy speaking to the country about the Cuban Missile Crisis

For the next four days, President Kennedy and Soviet Premier Khrushchev were engaged in intense diplomacy that left both sides on the brink. Europeans and Americans braced for potential war, wondering whether any day might be their last. During that time, however, the Soviets used back-channel communications through Attorney General Robert F. Kennedy seeking a way for both sides to reach an agreement and save face. Finally, on October 28th, Khrushchev and Kennedy agreed to the removal of the missiles, under U.N. supervision. In exchange, the U.S. vowed never to invade Cuba, while privately agreeing to remove intercontinental ballistic missiles (ICBMs) that had been stationed in Turkey, near the Soviet border, under the Eisenhower Administration. Realizing how close they had come to disaster, the Americans and Soviets agreed to establish a direct communication line, known as the "Hotline", between the two sides in an effort to avoid nuclear catastrophe resulting from miscommunication.

In addition to being one of the leading voices in support of a blockade, Bobby played a central role in defusing the crisis through back channels involving Soviet officials. At the height of the Cuban Missile Crisis, Bobby met regularly with the Soviet Ambassador in Washington to ensure that conversations between Kennedy and Khrushchev were genuine and meaningful. With his intimate knowledge of the situation, Bobby personally helped the President draft the plan for negotiations with the Soviets, which included removing American missiles from Turkey in exchange for the removal of Soviet missiles from Cuba. President Kennedy had created a committee, the Executive Committee (ExComm), and Attorney General Kennedy was placed on that Committee, giving him enormous influence over the President's decision during the defining moment of his Presidency.

After 13 days, the Cuban Missile Crisis came to a peaceful end, with the Soviets backing down from challenging the blockade, and war was averted. Though it was largely unknown at the time, the role Bobby played in the crisis was a critical one. He would later write a gripping account of the Cuban Missile Crisis, offering a detailed, inside look at how the Kennedy Administration handled the affair and reached a solution. That book, *Thirteen Days: A Memoir of the Cuban Missile Crisis*, was published a year after Bobby's assassination.

Despite the foreign policy failures of Kennedy's first year and a half in office, the Cuban Missile Crisis significantly increased the Administration's credibility on foreign policy matters. By fending off Soviet aggression, Kennedy renewed the America's commitment to defending the Western Hemisphere and repositioned the nation with strength. Prior to the crisis, the Soviets had viewed the Kennedy Administration as weak, especially for its timidity on Fidel Castro. The Cuban Missile Crisis was in part a result of Kennedy's prior failure; the Soviets thought they could push the Americans in Cuba. By averting nuclear war and removing the Soviet missiles from Cuba, President Kennedy's political popularity improved, and he was again lauded for his foreign policy achievements.

Senator Edward M. Kennedy

With brothers John and Bobby heading off to Washington in 1961, 29 year old Ted Kennedy had to bide his time between then and the Special Election of 1962 that he hoped would land him John's old seat in the U.S. Senate. Thus, Ted took a job as an assistant district attorney in Suffolk County, Massachusetts. The family's wealth and fortunes were so considerable at this point that Ted's salary was $1 a year.

Of course, Ted had his eye firmly fixed on 1962, and with that in mind, he made a handful of foreign visits, ostensibly improving his foreign policy bona fides for a future Senate Run. Though it was unknown at the time, one of Ted's trips to Latin America caught the FBI's attention. According to an internal FBI memo that was not made public until 2011, Kennedy rented out a brothel in Chile and used bordellos during the trip. He also met with people being investigated for ties to communism, and one woman who was being investigated as a potential Soviet spy. By the time the memo saw the light of day, the nation was quite aware of the Kennedy brothers' womanizing, a vice that has come to be inextricably tied with the Kennedy legacy. In reporting on the memo, the *Boston Globe* noted "it is unlikely to alter public opinion about a man whose triumphs and failings are already well known." Had anyone known of it in 1961, however, Ted's political career may have been over before it began.

In February 1962, Ted turned 30, making him eligible for the seat in the Senate. But despite the fact the special appointment had been made in order to pave the way for Ted to take the seat in 1962, others had no intention of simply handing it to him. Ted was challenged in the Democratic primary by Edward J. McCormack, Jr., the state's attorney general, and McCormack wasted no time hammering him. Arguing that a U.S. Senate seat "should be merited, and not inherited", McCormack asserted that if Kennedy's name was Edward Moore instead of Edward Moore Kennedy, is candidacy "would be a joke". With John and Bobby already in Washington, opponents asked voters, "Don't you think that Teddy is one Kennedy too many?" McCormack constantly reminded people through his campaign slogan, "I back Jack, but Teddy ain't ready"

Throughout the campaign, Ted found himself heavily scrutinized on all sides. A slew of attacks came out against him during his campaign, and the fact that he cheated at Harvard and had been suspended was revealed. Ted was branded an inexperienced, spoiled kid who thought himself entitled to the Senate seat by virtue of his last name. Sometimes Ted's campaign seemed to suggest they were right; his campaign slogan, "He can do more for Massachusetts", was the exact same slogan John had used in his first run for that same Senate seat 10 years earlier.

Nevertheless, Ted trounced McCormack by a nearly 2-1 margin, fueled in no small part by the Kennedy political machine and money. At the same time, Ted let the mud slung onto him drip right off, turning his youth and charisma into a political asset in his campaigning. In the general election, Kennedy's opponent, George Cabot Lodge, was the son of Henry Cabot Lodge, Jr., the former Massachusetts U.S. Senator that John had defeated in 1952. Because Ted's opponent would himself have been arguably "inheriting" the Senate seat based on his family name, the attacks of elitism against Kennedy largely ceased in the Fall. It was a contest between two wealthy "Boston Brahmins" in Massachusetts.

On Election Day, Ted defeated Lodge handedly, becoming the second Kennedy to defeat a Lodge for the seat. Furthermore, John had defeated Henry Cabot Lodge a second time, because Lodge was Nixon's Vice Presidential nominee in 1960. The Lodge-Kennedy competition continued to be one-sided.

Because the election was a special one, Ted was sworn in as U.S. Senator a day after his election. November 7, 1962 would be the first of over 16,000 days that Ted held the office. At 30 years old, however, the eventual Lion of the Senate was understandably deferential to old hands in the Senate, and he stuck his nose to the grindstone and immersed himself in behind the scenes Senate work on committees. At the time, Ted was obviously overshadowed by his older brothers, still very much the kid brother in Washington. Ted would assert that his brothers were superior in every conceivable way to him, and many might have accepted that in 1962. He was less articulate than Robert and less politically pragmatic than John, although his colleagues, like his earlier classmates, found him fun and likable.

Nuclear Testing and West Berlin

Throughout his presidency, John made repeated efforts to negotiate a treaty banning nuclear testing with the Soviets. At Vienna in June 1961, the young president held his ground until he and Khrushchev reached an informal agreement against nuclear weapons testing. While this was initially hailed as a success, it fell apart just months later when the Soviets began testing nuclear weapons in September, and began sending them to Cuba the following year. In 1962, after almost 40 months of negotiations led by the United Nations Disarmament Commission, negotiations between the U.S. and the Soviets again failed to come to an agreement on nuclear weapons testing.

By the summer of 1963, however, after nearly five years of talks, the U.S., Great Britain and the Soviet Union finally agree to a limited ban on nuclear testing. This treaty halted testing in the atmosphere, outer space and under water, but not underground. It was quickly ratified in Congress.

During that same summer, another East-West controversy had come to the fore: the Berlin Wall. Build in 1961 to prevent East Berliners from venturing into West Berlin, the Wall had come to serve as a symbol for global division.

In June of 1963, President Kennedy travelled to West Berlin, where he gave his famous Berlin Wall Speech. In it, he said "All free men, wherever they may live, are citizens of Berlin, and, therefore, as a free man, I take pride in the words: Ich bin ein Berliner." In the speech, Kennedy reiterated the American commitment to Berlin and West Germany. It was very well received by Germans, and it helped to solidify the alignment of Western Europe with the United States against the Soviets.

The Most Popular Woman in the World

By the middle of Kennedy's presidency, Jackie was popular across the world, to the extent that she provided a political asset at times where the president was coming under fire for certain policies and mishaps during the Cold War. Naturally, the Kennedy administration utilized Jackie's talents accordingly, and the media was all too happy to treat her as a star attraction.

On one trip to France, one of Jackie's favorite places, she wowed those who traveled with the Kennedys and those who visited with them. In one gushing article about Jackie on the trip, Time Magazine jokingly referred to the president as "that fellow who came with her." In another trip to the Middle East, she was presented with a horse. And to the consternation of some White House officials, Jackie was offered a puppy as a goodwill gesture by the Russians, worrying some advisors that the Russians might have somehow installed microphones in the puppy's body that could allow them to eavesdrop in the White House wherever the dog ran around.

In the years after the Kennedy presidency, friends and intimate observers would note that in public Jackie seemed to subdue just how bright she was in order to keep the spotlight intently fixed on the superficial aspects of being First Lady, from her style to her grace and manners. Given her education, and the fact that many people came away impressed by her intelligence after meeting her, it can be safely assumed that Jackie did so intentionally to help curry favor.

Jackie riding a camel in Pakistan

Jackie hosting a reception for wives of American Society of Newspaper Editors members.

Jackie played the role of hostess and happy face better than any First Lady in American history, successfully renovating the White House and other buildings, as well as managing entertainment in the White House itself. In early 1963, however, Jackie learned that she was once again pregnant, and she thus decided to restrict her work in the Executive Mansion. Having already suffered a miscarriage and stillborn child, and needing Caesarian sections to give birth to Caroline and John Jr., Jackie took much rest during her pregnancy. Few First Ladies had given birth while their husbands occupied the White House, though the event was not unprecedented. Jackie decided to follow the precedents set by those who came before her and take up rest and relaxation during her pregnancy rather than offer more news to the media.

The First Lady was due to deliver the third Kennedy child in mid-September. Five weeks earlier, she and her family stayed on Cape Cod, near the Kennedy family compound. It was a relaxing place for the family, which had spent many years vacationing in the area.

This vacation, however, would anything but relaxing. On August 7, 1963, Jackie went into premature labor, nearly 5 weeks earlier than her expected due date. She was sent to Otis Air Force Base, where she gave birth through an emergency Caesarian section. Unfortunately, because the infant boy, Patrick Bouvier Kennedy, was premature, his body was not fully developed. His lungs were not well developed, and the child died two days after he was born. A funeral mass was held in Boston the next day. He was buried alongside his sister, Arabella, in Holyhood Cemetery in Brookline, Massachusetts, where their father had been born. Like Arabella, Patrick's remains would later be reinterred at Arlington.

Jackie was devastated. She had lost another child, but this time, she did so with the eyes of the nation upon her. She was depressed and ambivalent about returning to the White House, despite all the work she had put into restoring the building.

November 22, 1963

The First Family had almost no time to cope with the loss of Patrick before tragedy hit even closer to home.

By November of 1963, President Kennedy was not overly popular nationwide. His foreign policy had a number of successes, but Americans had also not forgotten the failures of 1961 and early 1962. Furthermore, his tepid support of civil rights was dividing his own party, between liberals and conservatives. Southern conservatives thought Kennedy had proposed too much, while liberals didn't think voting rights went far enough. The strains would eventually undo the former Democratic coalition of the previous 80 years, done in with the help of Richard Nixon's "southern strategy" in the late 1960s, which saw the South turn solidly Republican at the expense of losing minority support.

Such division was already on display in the state of Texas, where the sitting governor was in conflict with his state's party over the issue. Liberal and conservative Democrats were divided there, which threatened to reduce President Kennedy's chances of carrying the state's 25 electoral votes in the 1964 election. John had already made Lyndon Johnson his running mate over the objections of his brother Bobby in 1960 in order to better his chances of winning Texas that year, which he barely did. It was clear how important Texas was to him, and as part of his reelection efforts the President travelled to the state to build support there, nearly an entire year before the presidential election. Formally, the purpose of the trip was to sew up differences within the state's Democratic Party, but no one doubted that John hoped to win some votes along the way.

Arriving in Dallas the morning of November 22, 1963

November 22, 1963 started as a typical Friday, and many Americans were unaware that President Kennedy was even heading to Dallas, Texas. John and Jackie arrived in Dallas in the morning, with Texas Governor Connally alongside them and Vice President Johnson due to arrive later to meet them there. The Kennedys and the Connallys intended to participate in public events later in the day, and Jackie and John were surprised by the warm reception they received. That day, Jackie opted to wear a bright pink Chanel suit for the occasion, a conspicuously fashionable choice even for her. Knowing full well that the country and press viewed her every fashion style with interest and fascination, Jackie fully intended to flatter with it.

A public parade was hosted for the President and First Lady on November 22nd, and the First Couple rode in an open motorcade en route to a speech Kennedy would deliver later. The Kennedys sat in the back seat, and in front of them were the Connallys. Things had gone so well in his meetings with Democratic officials and in the reception they had received that President Kennedy chose to keep the presidential limousine's top down, in order to feel more connected to the public that had lined the streets in anticipation of seeing the motorcade drive by. As they waved to the people lining the streets, around 12:30 p.m. Central Standard Time, Governor Connally's wife turned around to the first couple and said, "Mr. President, you can't say Dallas doesn't love you."

As the Presidential Motorcade entered Dealey Plaza, it turned onto Elm Street and came into the sightlines of a sixth floor window at the School Depository building. There, Lee Harvey Oswald, a Communist sympathizer, had set up a sniper's nest with a high-powered rifle. With the motorcade traveling at low speed, Oswald missed with his first shot, causing everyone in the motorcade to notice. However, the next shot hit Kennedy in the upper back, traveled through his body, and struck Governor Connally's arm in the front passenger seat. The bullet would come to be referred to by conspiracy theorists as the "Magic Bullet".

At the time, Jackie initially thought there was a malfunction in the vehicle, not realizing what had happened until Governor Connally turned around and screamed. At that moment, Jackie created an indelible image by leaning in closer to her husband, who was grasping at his neck. As President Kennedy hunched over, Oswald's next shot missed the motorcade, but his next shot was a direct hit that shattered Kennedy's skull. Panicked and in shock, Jackie bolted onto the rear of the car towards the Secret Service Agent standing on the bumper as the president slumped over with an obviously fatal wound. Clint Hill, the agent, later said he thought Mrs. Kennedy was reaching for a piece of the President's skull that had been blasted off in the attack.

Kennedy was rushed to the nearest hospital, Parkland Hospital in Dallas and immediately entered a Trauma Room, where doctors began operating. From the start, though, everyone realized the President would not survive. The First Lady demanded to be let into the operating room, wanting to be with her husband when he died. Though she was initially denied, doctors relented and allowed her in. A priest was also called in to administer last rites. At 1:00 p.m. Central Standard Time, the President was declared dead. With that, Mrs. Kennedy put her wedding ring on her husband's finger, he was loaded into a casket, and together they boarded Air Force One.

Aside from the spectators who turned out to greet Kennedy and his wife at Dealey Plaza, some of the first people to find out about the shooting in Dallas were those watching the soap opera *As the World Turns* on CBS. In the middle of the show, around 1:30 p.m. EST, Walter Cronkite cut in with a CBS News Bulletin, announcing that President Kennedy had been shot at and was severely wounded.

The news began to spread across offices and schools across the country, with teary-eyed teachers having to inform their schoolchildren of the shooting in Dallas. Most Americans left school and work early and headed home to watch the news. Even the normally stoic Cronkite couldn't hide his emotions. Around 1:40 p.m. Central Standard Time, misty eyed and with his voice choked up, Cronkite delivered the news that the president was dead.

At the time, Ted was the Senate's Presiding Officer. While performing the duties of presiding over the parliamentarian procedures of the Senate, an aide rushed in to inform the Senator that his brother had been shot in Texas. With Bobby busy comforting Jackie, the task of informing Joseph Sr. fell to Ted. After learning of his brother's death, Ted flew to Hyannisport, Massachusetts, the site of the Kennedy Compound.

Only a few years earlier, Joseph Sr. had a stroke, and by 1963 he was frail and ill. Thus, the task of telling him of his son's death was an even harder one. Ted reportedly had some difficulty with relaying the information, telling his father that "there's been a bad accident. The President had been hurt very badly. In fact, he died." With that, Joseph Sr. outstretched his arms while he and Teddy wept. Joseph Sr. had longed for a Presidential son. He had achieved it, but the dream ended abruptly and unexpectedly on November 22nd, 1963.

That day, stunned Americans wondered if the assassination was a Soviet conspiracy, a Cuban conspiracy, or the actions of a lone nut. Oswald was arrested hours after Kennedy's shooting, after he shot and killed Officer J.D. Tippit. In fact, Oswald was initially arrested for Tippit's death, not Kennedy's, and he claimed he was a "patsy" who had killed neither man. Two days later, Oswald was being transported through the basement of the police's headquarters when nightclub owner Jack Ruby stepped out of the crowd and shot Oswald point blank in the chest, killing him on live TV. The Warren Commission later investigated the Kennedy assassination and ruled that Oswald was the lone assassin, but the bizarre sequence of events have ensured that the Kennedy assassination is still widely considered one of the great mysteries of American history, with conspiracy theories accusing everyone from Fidel Castro to the mob of orchestrating a hit.

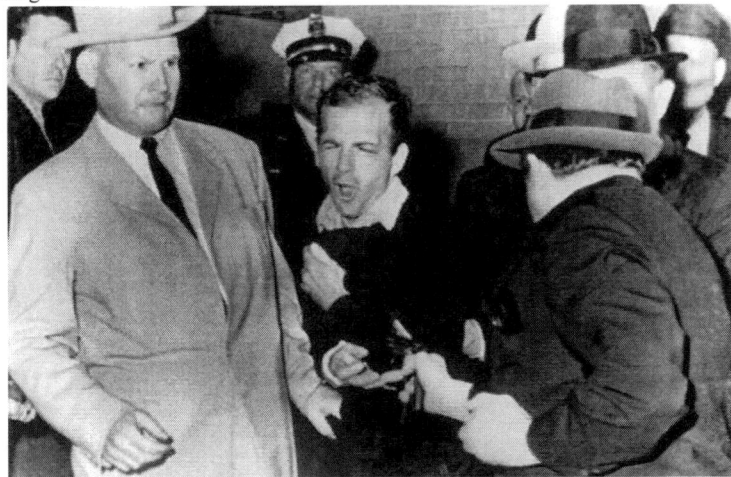

Ruby shooting Oswald

Leading the Nation in Mourning

Aboard Air Force One, Jackie stood next to Lyndon Johnson as he was sworn in as President of the United States at 2:38 p.m. Central Standard Time. Noticeably, Jackie continued to wear her pink outfit, which was still full of her husband's blood, and though she washed her face and hair (something she later claimed she regretted), parts of John's skull were still on her.

President Kennedy's body was brought back to the White House, where it rested in repose in the East Room for 24 hours, draped in an American flag. Two Roman Catholic priests prayed at the side of the body, while military guards stood in formation around it. Jackie refused to leave her husband's body until the priests were present. These hours in the East Room were for private viewings only.

After that period, on Sunday, Kennedy's body was taken to the U.S. Capitol Rotunda, where it lied in state. About 300,000 people came to Washington to watch the procession from the White House to the Capitol, which included a horse drawn carriage. Because no funeral plans were drawn up prior to Kennedy's death, the precedent set by Abraham Lincoln's assassination was used as a model. Dignitaries from around the world and within the U.S. attended Kennedy's funeral, including all surviving presidents except Herbert Hoover, who was too ill to attend (and died months later).

From there, the President's body was brought from the Capitol to St. Matthew's Cathedral for a complete funeral. Throughout the funeral, Ted and Bobby played important and visible roles in helping lead both the Kennedy family and the nation through the grieving process. They were with Jackie at all critical moments, and helped organize and ensure that the state funeral went as smoothly as possible. The three of them had to visit the rotunda and escort the President's body out of the Capitol.

Mrs. Kennedy walked with both of her children as the procession moved to St. Matthew's. Famously, she instructed John Kennedy Jr. to salute his father's coffin as it passed. Sadly, his third birthday, November 25, 1963, coincided with the funeral. Deemed too young to attend the burial, the salute would be John Jr.'s final goodbye to his father.

After the funeral Mass, President Kennedy's body was taken to Arlington National Cemetery for burial. At the end of the burial service, Jackie lit the eternal flame that continues to burn above the President's grave to this day. That famous tribute to Kennedy's memory was his wife's idea.

Chapter 7: Two Senator Kennedys

Jackie Leaves Washington

The turmoil of Kennedy's assassination left an uncertain future for Jackie and her two children, who were still just 6 and 3 years old. The family remained in the White House for two weeks, gathering their personal items and preparing for what promised to be a rocky transition to civilian life.

She may not have been First Lady after November 22, 1963, but Jackie was hardly going to be disappearing from the spotlight either. Just a week after her husband's death, Jackie was interviewed briefly by *Life* Magazine. In that interview, she used the term "Camelot" to refer admiringly to the short, but promising, Kennedy Presidency, forever changing the history surrounding her husband. In the interview, she said her husband had listened frequently to the title song of King Arthur's Camelot before heading to sleep. With that, she compared her husband's Presidency to the Monarchy of King Arthur, which was tragically cut short, despite the promise it held for the future.

As the country now knows today, Camelot was certainly more myth than reality. Behind the façade of a vibrant young President was a man with a broken body, and Kennedy was taking multiple drugs on a daily basis just to manage the pain before his assassination. And Jackie was personally aware of the fact that the seemingly picture perfect First Family was a myth. It was a well known fact that President Kennedy was a philandering womanizer, never more poignantly put on public display than when Marilyn Monroe seductively sang "Happy Birthday, Mr. President" to him in 1962. Even today, in an age where extramarital affairs instantly ruin political careers, Kennedy's adultery is remembered more like part of the Kennedy package than as a character flaw. Jackie knew full well that her husband engaged rampantly in extramarital affairs, but she had no recourse but to put on a happy face.

Upon leaving the White House, Jackie, Caroline and John Jr. lived briefly in their home in Georgetown in Washington. Publicly, she had portrayed a stoic widow, helping the nation in its grief, but privately she was a broken woman. By 1964, Jackie became worried about the privacy of her children, which was impossible inside the Beltway. She also found Washington intolerable, unable to escape all the memories of her husband. Leaving for New York City, where she purchased an apartment on Fifth Avenue in Manhattan, she hoped never to see the White House again and went out of her way to avoid all sight of her one time home for the rest of her life. She spent much of the next year in mourning, both for her husband and her lost son Patrick. Caroline later noted that her mother cried frequently throughout 1964.

While Jackie might have wanted to forget Washington D.C., she did not want to forget her husband, nor did she want the world to forget him. For much of the rest of the decade, Jackie carried on like a family dignitary, memorializing her husband at several events across the country and Europe. In 1967, she participated in the commissioning of the U.S. Navy Aircraft Carrier, the *USS John F. Kennedy*. She dedicated memorials to Kennedy in England and Ireland, and she helped establish the John F. Kennedy Library in Boston, which now holds some of her life's most famous artifacts in addition to Kennedy's presidential papers.

June 19, 1964

Like Jackie, Bobby and Ted took the assassination hard. Since the earliest days of John's presidential campaign, the brothers had become personally closer than they ever had before. Together, they had built something of a family dynasty, and they seemed to be on the path of forging a family legacy and identity that was unprecedented in the United States. Losing the central pillar devastated the family both personally and professionally.

After the president's death, the Kennedy family had to rally around each other, with both the two surviving brothers, Jackie, and the young families all coming closer together. But they had only half a year to cope before Ted nearly lost his own life in a plane crash in western Massachusetts on June 19, 1964.

Along with Indiana Senator Birch Bayh, the pair was headed for Massachusetts, where Ted was to begin his campaign for re-election in the regularly-scheduled 1964 Massachusetts Senate Election. Due to bad weather, however, the plane crashed in Southampton, Massachusetts, en route to a small airport in Westfield.

Although Senate Bayh and his wife were only slightly injured, the plane's pilot and one of Senator Kennedy's aides were killed. Meanwhile, Senator Kennedy was severely wounded, and amid the wreckage, he was pinned and could not eject himself from the plane. Senator Bayh had to personally pull Ted from the aircraft, and everyone involved was quickly brought to a hospital. Given Ted's injuries, his survival was nearly miraculous. He had suffered a severe back injury, a punctured lung, broken ribs, and internal bleeding. The injuries sustained in the plane crash would cause him chronic pain for the rest of his life.

Ted spent the next few months in the hospital recovering and was unable to actively campaign, but being an incumbent with the name Kennedy in 1964 was campaigning enough. Ted's wife Joan did most of the campaigning on his behalf, and Kennedy defeated his Republican opponent by a 3-to-1 margin. Like his brother John, who had studied politics while recuperating from back surgery to write *Profiles in Courage* about some of America's greatest Senators, Ted spent his convalescence studying the minutiae of certain issues, including the country's health care system, which he would later come to dub "the cause of my life."

Senator Robert F. Kennedy

As the Kennedy Family staggered back to its feet in the wake of John's death, Bobby took the assassination as an opportunity to fight for and ultimately reshape the Kennedy Legacy. With his brother's death, he became more reflective on the purpose of the Kennedy family. What was their goal?

With that, Bobby began an era, along with Ted, of articulating what it was the Kennedys stood for. Among the most important elements was a strong stand on Civil Rights, which had now become an important element of Bobby's own personal plank. Additionally, support for a modest expansion of the New Deal to help the poor and the needy was a defining aspect of the Kennedy identity. Overall, a broad progressive program became the rallying cry of the Kennedy Family.

At first, Bobby decided to try to uphold his brother's legacy in the new President's Cabinet, where he would continue to serve as Attorney General. The wind had been taken out of Bobby's sails after his brother's assassination, but he was still, after all, Attorney General when Vice President Johnson succeeded the dead president.

However, the animus between Johnson and Bobby had persisted, and Bobby's time in the Johnson Administration proved to be short lived. Long having been on unfriendly terms with the now-sitting President, Kennedy was unable to forge better personal relations with President Johnson. Their bad relationship, of course, had its origins in the earliest days of 1960 Presidential Campaign, when Bobby opposed Johnson's nomination for Vice President.

Even when President Kennedy was still alive, Johnson and Bobby Kennedy's relationship had further deteriorated. What began as a one-sided dislike on Bobby's end became mutual. Johnson held high hopes for the Vice Presidency, hoping to wield significant power in the White House and in Washington. As is often the case, however, Vice President Johnson was largely forgotten while Kennedy was President. The Attorney General was more intimately involved in the important moments of the Kennedy Presidency, sparking enmity from Vice President Johnson that further weakened their relationship.

As the 1964 election approached, there was some talk among the media that Robert Kennedy was a good fit for the Vice Presidency, and that Johnson should choose him as a running mate. Politically it made sense, since the Kennedy name was naturally revered in the wake of the assassination. At the Democratic National Convention that year, Bobby received a standing ovation that lasted over 20 minutes. Internally at the White House, however, neither Johnson nor Kennedy was interested in the arrangement. The two now bitterly disliked each other and would have nothing of the idea.

By 1964, Bobby was disillusioned with work at the White House. In his mind, he compared Lyndon Johnson to the previous President Johnson: Andrew Johnson, who assumed the Presidency after Lincoln's assassination and largely defied his predecessor's views on Reconstruction and Civil Rights. Bobby thought Lyndon Johnson, a Southerner, would turn back the dial on the Kennedy legacy.

Kennedy's assessments would prove premature (and incorrect), but he had made up his mind. Seeking political influence from outside the White House, Bobby resigned as Attorney General and threw his hat into the ring for a U.S. Senate election in New York. Bobby certainly had plenty of experience in political campaigning, but the 1964 election provided unique circumstances. By running for the Senate from New York after having not lived there for the past few years, Bobby's Republican opponent accused him of being a carpetbagger. Bobby also faced a Republican incumbent, Senator Kenneth Keating, who was running for his first reelection.

The bulk of the campaign focused on Kennedy's devotion to New York. Was he genuinely interested in serving the people of New York, or did he just have higher ambitions, perhaps the Presidency itself? According to Keating, the people of New York did not want to be used as a springboard for one man's ambitions. Bobby responded to this accusation, noting that his opponent may have lived in New York the longest and had the best New York accent, but that Kennedy was the most qualified and the most in line with the political beliefs of the people of New York. Furthermore, he wasn't exactly an outsider in New York; he went to school there as a child and lived there prior to becoming Attorney General. The state was his most recent home, and he hadn't lived there any less than any other state in the Union, though his name was obviously intimately associated with Massachusetts.

At the end of the campaign, New Yorkers evidently didn't find Bobby's citizenship to be an issue. He won the election decisively, winning nearly 54% of the vote, compared to his next nearest opponent's 43%. Senator Robert F. Kennedy was inaugurated in early 1965, giving him the platform outside the White House that he had desired. That year, he joined his brother in the Senate, who was representing Massachusetts, marking an historic moment when two brothers served in the U.S. Senate at the same time.

With Bobby's election to the Senate, Ted's significance in the upper house of the Congress was overshadowed by his more eloquent and famous brother. With the passion surrounding John Kennedy's memory and "Camelot", it was up to Ted and Bobby to be the standard bearer for the Kennedy family. Since he was the older and far more experienced brother, it was Bobby who became the leader of the family.

Much as he had as Attorney General, Senator Kennedy aligned himself with African-Americans and their movement with Civil Rights. More broadly, he took the lessons of the Civil Rights Movement and incorporated them on a global stage, emphasizing the importance of human rights everywhere on earth.

In June 1966, Senator Kennedy inaugurated this approach with a visit to South Africa. There, he personally observed South Africa's apartheid system, which was all too familiar with the segregation across the South in the United States. On June 6, he gave one of the most famous speeches of his life before a crowd in Cape Town. Pondering the meaning of human rights and their importance in a civilized world, Kennedy told the crowd:

"At the heart of that Western freedom and democracy is the belief that the individual man, the child of God, is the touchstone of value, and all society, groups, the state, exist for his benefit. Therefore the enlargement of liberty for individual human beings must be the supreme goal and the abiding practice of any Western society… Many nations have set forth their own definitions and declarations of these principles. And there have often been wide and tragic gaps between promise and performance, ideal and reality. Yet the great ideals have constantly recalled us to our duties. And - with painful slowness - we have extended and enlarged the meaning and the practice of freedom for all our people… "Give me a place to stand," said Archimedes, "and I will move the world." These men moved the world, and so can we all. Few will have the greatness to bend history itself, but each of us can work to change a small portion of events, and in the total of all those acts will be written the history of this generation. Thousands of Peace Corps volunteers are making a difference in isolated villages and city slums in dozens of countries. Thousands of unknown men and women in Europe resisted the occupation of the Nazis and many died, but all added to the ultimate strength and freedom of their countries. It is from numberless diverse acts of courage and belief that human history is shaped. *Each time a man stands up for an ideal, or acts to improve the lot of others, or strikes out against injustice, he sends forth a tiny ripple of hope, and crossing each other from a million different centers of energy and daring those ripples build a current which can sweep down the mightiest walls of oppression and resistance.*"

.On the home front, Bobby continued to champion federal intervention on behalf of African-Americans. He was a staunch supporter of the Voting Rights Act of 1965, which strengthened federal protection of the right to vote. He also visited some of the nation's poorest regions, often populated densely by African-Americans. This included a visit to the Mississippi Delta Region, where he assessed the effectiveness of the War on Poverty.

Kennedy's language was more fervently progressive than his older brother's. While John Kennedy was often hailed as a moderate – he was even opposed by the Democratic Party's more liberal wing in 1960 – Bobby, along with Ted, reinvigorated the Kennedy brand, allying it staunchly with liberalism and progressivism. Together, the two Senators spoke passionately about the disaffected and the excluded, whether they were African-Americans, immigrants, Native Americans or the poor. Both Ted and Bobby became firm populists during these days in the Senate.

Chapter 8: 1968

Vietnam

During President Kennedy's administration, a smaller crisis than the one in Cuba began to grow, beginning with the French fighting communist rebels in the southeast Asian colony of French Indochina. After a bloody counterinsurgency campaign by the French failed, France separated its colony into two parts: North Vietnam, which would be a pro-communist state, and South Vietnam, which was aligned with the West. However, South Vietnam quickly became embroiled in its own guerrilla war against communist insurgents who wanted to join it with North Vietnam.

President Kennedy, following President Truman's containment policy, offered limited aid to South Vietnam to prevent it from falling into communist hands. After President Kennedy's assassination, however, President Johnson determined that only direct U.S. military assistance would prevent South Vietnam from falling to communists, which had support from both China and the Soviet Union. Thus, Johnson ordered U.S. navy ships to the area.

On August 2, 1964, the USS Maddox was patrolling in the Gulf of Tonkin when it was fired upon by North Vietnamese torpedo boats. Though no Americans were hurt, naval crews were on heightened alert. Two days later, the Maddox and USS Turner Joy were certain they were being followed by hostile North Vietnamese boats, and both fired at targets popping up on their radar.

After that second "encounter," now known as the Gulf of Tonkin Incident, President Johnson approved air strikes against the North Vietnamese, and Congress approved military action with the Gulf of Tonkin Resolution. By the end of the year, over 15,000 Americans had been stationed in South Vietnam. It would be years before the government revealed that the second encounter was no encounter at all. The government never did figure out what the Maddox and Turner Joy were firing at that night, but there was no evidence to suggest it involved North Vietnamese forces.

Nevertheless, after the Gulf of Tonkin, President Johnson ordered air strikes against North Vietnam. For the next several years, North Vietnam was the most bombed place on the planet, as American bombers dropped tons and tons of bombs on the "Ho Chi Minh Trail." But the Viet Cong kept coming. Johnson had sent fewer than 5,000 Marines to Vietnam in early 1965, but he quickly upped it to 200,000 by the end of the year. There was no going back.

Like many of the personal rifts between the Bobby and the President, Senator Kennedy disagreed with Johnson's foreign policy, especially as it related to Vietnam and Southeast Asia. As Attorney General, Bobby had supported his brother's initial interventions in Vietnam as part of the broader Cold War. Kennedy agreed with his brother that communist expansion needed to be halted, which was the basic premise of the United States' Cold War foreign policy stretching from Cuba to Asia.

Where Bobby departed from the Johnson Administration, however, was in its commitment to launch ground troops into Vietnam. This, Kennedy thought, was unnecessary and unlikely to be productive or successful. Additionally, Kennedy gradually began to move towards a stance that integrated human rights as a central component of U.S. foreign policy; bombing the Vietnamese countryside and killing innocent civilians was not consistent with this view.

Initially, Kennedy chose to only privately caution the Johnson Administration against its decision. However, in 1967, shortly after Martin Luther King took the same stance, Bobby came out publicly against the Vietnam War, calling for a full-blown withdrawal. His opposition coincided with a rising public movement against the war, and increasing outrage with the Johnson Presidency. Finally, Kennedy's full blown rift with Johnson was public, which showed the fissures in the Democratic Party entering 1968.

Bobby Runs for President

By 1968, Bobby had utilized his platform in the Senate to open up a rift in the Democratic Party. On the one side were the Kennedy's, including Ted, and the anti-Vietnam War activists. On the other was the sitting President Lyndon Johnson, and those who supported the ongoing War in Vietnam.

Bobby and Ted were always close, and they grew closer during their four years together in the Senate. When Bobby began flirting with the idea of a Presidential run, however, Ted initially advised his brother against the idea. Ironically, Ted thought it was not viable to run against an incumbent President, advice he would later ignore himself. Furthermore, it was a remarkable departure from standard political precedent, and Ted thought it was a risky one that threatened to lessen the Kennedy "brand."

Although hundreds of thousands protested the war in 1967, including Martin Luther King, Jr., a majority of the public still supported it, due in large part to the Johnson's administration public confidence. But as General Westmoreland talked of victory at the end of 1967, the Viet Cong launched a massive assault across South Vietnam in January 1968. Known as the Tet Offensive, the Viet Cong suffered hundreds of thousands of casualties, and the American forces never lost a battle. But American support for the war still plummeted.

As the Tet Offensive raged in Vietnam, Kennedy began to think seriously about running for the Presidency of the United States, a move that would put him on the same path as his elder brother. Tet was politically untenable for Johnson, and weakened his chances at reelection. But Bobby wasn't completely convinced. Seeking to defeat an incumbent President within his own political party was a political rarity. Few in American history had ever seriously sought such a victory.

By the end of 1967, however, Senator Kennedy wasn't the only Democratic considering replacing the unpopular Johnson. Senator Eugene McCarthy of Minnesota, long a leader of the anti-Vietnam War Movement, threw his hat into the race. To the surprise of the nation, he was only narrowly defeated in the first-in-the-nation primary in New Hampshire on March 12th. The sitting President of the United States had won the New Hampshire Primary with only a razor-thin margin of victory. Though Johnson had won the primary, the close margin made him appear vulnerable, an unusual position for a sitting president.

After McCarthy's close shave in New Hampshire, Bobby judged the time was right to enter the race. At the same time, however, Bobby sought to carry forward the Kennedy name, and with "Camelot" still fresh in America's minds, he declared his candidacy for the Presidency of the

United States. Bobby announced his candidacy from the same location where his brother had announced his own eight years earlier, in the Russell Senate Office Building in Washington. The McCarthy Campaign charged that he was an opportunist, relying on McCarthy's initial candidacy before declaring its own. Regardless, the Kennedy name continued to attract Americans across the country, and Bobby represented another chance at Camelot.

Kennedy's candidacy, as well as McCarthy's, indicated the deep division within the Democratic Party over the Vietnam War. On the one side was President Johnson, while Kennedy and McCarthy together split the anti-war vote. The pro-war Democrats lost their leader on March 31st, when President Johnson made an historic move and announced he would no longer seek renomination for the Presidency of the United States. Johnson was consumed by the Vietnam War while in the White House, and had little time to campaign. He never left the White House during the New Hampshire campaign, and feared that a long and brutal primary campaign, along with an equally onerous general election campaign, would sink his Presidency and his chances of winning. With McCarthy's near win in New Hampshire, Johnson began to harbor second thoughts about running in 1968.

President Johnson

Under Johnson, the Democratic Party had divided deeply. The Party divided into roughly four groups, some of which deeply despised the other factions. Johnson and his Vice President, Hubert Humphrey, were supported by labor unions and party bosses – what might be called the "party establishment." McCarthy attracted support primarily from white students who opposed the Vietnam War. Bobby was popular among Catholics and minority voters, including African-Americans and Hispanics. A fourth group, Southern segregationists, was threatening to bolt the Democratic Party altogether, and they tossed their support behind George C. Wallace of Alabama, who eventually decided to run for President without the Democratic Party's support.

With this framework, Johnson soon realized that the being renominated would be a tough battle, and on a personal note, he was concerned that his health was waning and that he would not survive another full term. On March 31st, 1968, Johnson thus shocked the nation by announcing, ahead of the Wisconsin primary, where polls showed him trailing badly, that he would not seek reelection for the Presidency of the United States.

The Democratic Nomination was now a race between two people: Kennedy and McCarthy. This bipolar race was a brief moment, however, when Vice President Humphrey decided to run for the Presidency. He garnered much of the "establishment" support that Johnson had won, and with the infrastructure of the party behind him, was favored to win enough delegates at the national convention.

The Democratic Primaries and the Assassination of Martin Luther King, Jr.

In 1968, the process of electing a nominee was not as well established as it is today. Not all states held a primary; at the time, only 13 states held primaries. Humphrey, the eventual nominee, did not even place his name on the ballot for any primary. Instead, party leaders – delegates – fought out the nomination at the convention floor.

Initially, Bobby decided on a strategy of working the party elders to gain support, while McCarthy focused on primaries. This worked to McCarthy's advantage, causing Kennedy to switch strategy. While Johnson won the New Hampshire primary, his exit from the race allowed McCarthy to win the next four, by wide margins: Wisconsin, Pennsylvania, Massachusetts and Washington, DC. McCarthy's victory in Massachusetts was especially damaging, given Kennedy's origins in the state.

The Kennedy campaign thus decided to contest the primaries, beginning with the state of Indiana. It would be in Indiana that Kennedy delivered yet another one of his most famous speeches. On the night of April 3, 1968, Dr. Martin Luther King, Jr. addressed an audience at the Mason Temple in Memphis, Tennessee. King was in the city on behalf of black sanitation workers who were on strike due to discrimination. No stranger to death threats, King told listeners that night, "I've seen the Promised Land. I may not get there with you. But I want you to know tonight, that we, as a people, will get to the Promised Land." Less than 24 hours later, King was standing on the balcony of his hotel room, Room 306 at the Lorraine Hotel, when a single shot rang out. King had been hit in the face by a sniper's bullet, and emergency surgery failed to save his life. King was pronounced dead at 7:00 p.m.

On the night of April 4, 1968, America burned, literally. As news of King's assassination spread, race riots erupted across hundreds of cities in the United States. Among the country's major cities, one of the few that did not experience riots was Indianapolis. That night, Bobby was in town to hold a political rally, but after hearing of King's death he chose to make brief, impromptu comments instead of a campaign speech. Speaking for less than five minutes, he told the crowd, "What we need in the United States is not division; what we need in the United States is not hatred; what we need in the United States is not violence or lawlessness, but love and wisdom, and compassion toward one another, and a feeling of justice towards those who still suffer within our country, whether they be white or whether they be black."

Bobby's speech is often credited for calming tensions in the city that night, but he had only been there in the first place as part of a new campaign strategy to begin running in the primaries.

McCarthy's campaign had gained significant media momentum from his victories in the state primaries, and Bobby hoped to steal that away. Some of his advisors thought the strategy was a risky one. If he lost, his campaign would lose steam, whereas by not contesting, Bobby could say that McCarthy's wins were insignificant. However, Kennedy decided to campaign in primaries, beginning with Indiana. His strategy proved fruitful, when he won the state with 42% of the vote to McCarthy's 27%.

With that, Bobby's campaign claimed momentum and moved on to the next state: Nebraska. A win there, Kennedy hoped, would embolden his campaign and give him a significant lead in the upcoming delegate-rich California primary. Bobby's hopes materialized when he won Nebraska, with a majority of the vote. He had now proved that his appeal was not limited to Catholics and racial minorities, and his campaign was not just a fringe 'issue" candidacy; it was a legitimate one. Those following the Kennedy campaign couldn't help but notice the extent to which his supporters revered Bobby, as he generated enthusiasm on a seemingly unprecedented level that summer. Aides would later recall the difficulty they had even moving Bobby and wife Ethel away from the onrush of crowds after he would finish speaking.

The Assassination of Robert F. Kennedy

June 4, 1968, was an important day for the Democratic nomination. Three states voted to allocate their delegates that day: California, New Jersey and South Dakota. With the results of Nebraska, Indiana and all the other primaries, Bobby's campaign began to forge better relationships with McCarthy. Bobby began to claim that Johnson and Humphrey's pro-Vietnam policies had been unequivocally repudiated: over 80% of the primary voters had voted for either McCarthy or Kennedy. This point was, perhaps, exaggerated, seeing as no pro-Vietnam candidate contested the primaries.

Regardless, Kennedy's message was a powerful one, and he now had his eye on the biggest prize of all the primary states: California. A win there would solidify his lead in the primary delegate count and give his candidacy added strength going into the convention. The other states voting that night were South Dakota and New Jersey. Bobby was expected to win big in South Dakota, as he did, while New Jersey's large labor and Democratic establishment vote won that state for McCarthy.

California, however, went Kennedy's way, giving him 46% of its vote to McCarthy's 42%. The results took hours to trail in, and the close nature of the primary meant Bobby was unable to give his victory speech until after midnight, in the early morning hours of June 5th, 1968. Amid much excitement, Kennedy gave a victory speech at the Ambassador Hotel in Los Angeles. Kennedy's campaign, which had initially seemed like a long shot, was gaining momentum. His victory in California gave him a convincing argument to bring the Democratic Convention, and significantly increased his chances of winning the nomination. Kennedy finished the speech with the words, "And now it's on to Chicago and let's win there."

After the speech, the plan was for Bobby to walk through the ballroom, where supporters had gathered. However, his aides wanted to quickly usher him to a press conference, and they were well aware of how difficult it could be to pry the public away from Bobby, and vice versa.

Instead, a way was cleared for Kennedy to move through the hotel's kitchen.

As Kennedy went through the kitchen and into a hall, he shook hands with people as they gathered around him. As he shook hands with a 17 year old busboy named Juan Romero, a 24 year old Jordanian named Sirhan Sirhan walked up to Bobby and began firing a .22 caliber revolver at him point blank. With bullets hitting him in the head and chest, Kennedy somehow remained conscious in the seconds after the shooting, asking Romero if everyone was safe as Romero knelt beside him and handed him a rosary. Given his injuries, it was miraculous that Kennedy survived 26 hours before dying the next morning, June 6, 1968. Bobby had tragically become the second Kennedy in less than a decade to be assassinated, and only the second sitting Senator in history to be killed.

Sirhan Sirhan

After making enemies with organized labor, Bobby had incurred the wrath of organized crime, cracking down on mobs as Attorney General in his brother's administration. Despite making these powerful enemies (with some conspiracy theorists believing the mob was involved in President Kennedy's death), Bobby was apparently assassinated by Sirhan Sirhan because he had expressed support for Israel throughout the '60s, including during the Six Day War in 1967. Sirhan Sirhan was an ardent advocate of the Palestinian cause and was angered by Kennedy's stance on the Middle East conflict.

After the assassination, authorities searching Sirhan Sirhan's residence found what appeared to be the ravings of a madman. "My determination to eliminate RFK is becoming more and more of an unshakable obsession. RFK must die. RFK must be killed. Robert F. Kennedy must be assassinated...Robert F. Kennedy must be assassinated before 5 June 68." Indeed, by shooting Kennedy on June 5, 1968, Sirhan Sirhan assassinated him on the first anniversary of the start of the Six Day War.

Bobby Kennedy's body was brought to St. Patrick's Cathedral in New York, where he lay in repose for several days before a funeral mass was held. It was left to younger brother Ted to eulogize his brother:

> "My brother need not be idealized, or enlarged in death beyond what he was in life; to be remembered simply as a good and decent man, who saw wrong and tried to right it, saw suffering and tried to heal it, saw war and tried to stop it. Those of us who loved him and who take him to his rest today, pray that what he was to us and what he wished for others will someday come to pass for all the world. As he said many times, in many parts of this nation, to those he touched and who sought to touch him: 'Some men see things as they are and say why. I dream things that never were and say why not.'"

With those words, Ted forever defined not only his brother's legacy, but the very meaning of being a Kennedy. As the last remaining Kennedy brother, the onus was now on the Senator from Massachusetts to live that definition to the fullest, ensuring that righting wrongs, healing suffering and stopping wars became the purpose of his life.

After the funeral, Bobby's body was taken to Washington D.C. by train, with mourners coming from across the nation to line tracks to see the train. Eventually, Bobby was buried next to John in Arlington National Cemetery.

Bobby's headstone in Arlington National Cemetery

"Jackie O"

While 1963 was among the worst years in Jackie's life, 1968 was a roller coaster year for Jackie personally and America as a whole. Bobby's death stunned Jackie. For the first time, the media began to speculate on the existence of a "Kennedy Curse," in which all Kennedys were at risk. In addition to the assassinations of John and Bobby, Ted had nearly died in a plane crash in 1964, which killed the pilot and even his aide. After Bobby's death, Jackie began to feel more vulnerable, concerned that her children would become targets of crazed fanatics. On a private level, Bobby's death represented a great loss to her, as she had become even closer to her brother-in-law following the death of her husband. Even with John gone, she was still a Kennedy.

Jackie felt she needed someone to protect her and her family after Bobby's death, saying, "If they're killing Kennedys, then my children are targets. I want to get out of this country." She found comfort found this in a Greek shipping magnate named Aristotle Onassis. In the summer of 1968, just months after Bobby's death, Jackie announced her engagement to Onassis. The announcement stunned everybody. Onassis was a wealthy businessman who even owned a private island and could clearly provide the security Jackie wanted, but he was almost 70 years old (and almost 30 years older than Jackie), and he had a reputation for personal and business immorality. In fact, Onassis' first marriage had ended after he cheated on his wife. At first glance, or any glance for that matter, it seemed an odd match between the impeccably mannered Jackie and the seemingly crude Greek magnate.

Onassis

However, Jackie found support in a seemingly unlikely place: the Kennedy family. The Kennedys approved of Jackie's decision, understanding her need for comfort, security and protection. Furthermore, Jackie felt safer spending some time abroad with her children in Greece, where the Kennedy name was not as well known. The two were married on October 20th, 1968, on the Greek island of Skorpios, which Onassis privately owned. The lack of glamour was startlingly different from Jackie's earlier marriage to John.

Much as the media speculated, Jackie's marriage to Aristotle Onassis was one of convenience, not happiness. Jackie was content with the temporary safety and security, but her relationship with Onassis was severely strained. It is reported that the couple considered divorcing early on in their marriage. Moreover, personal tragedy seemed to follow Jackie. When Onassis' son died in a plane accident shortly after the marriage, his daughter Cristina bought into fears about the "Kennedy Curse," believing it had spread from John to Jackie to the Onassis family itself. Though the idea was horribly superstitious, it added another issue to an already strained marriage.

Divorce did not need to materialize, however, when Aristotle died in 1975, making Jackie a widow for a second time. After his death, Jackie reportedly claimed no regrets about her marriage to the man. It had, after all, achieved what she hoped it would: a sense of security and peace after the turbulence of the 1960's. Her children were safe, and so was she. Of course, there was speculation that she had married him for the money, but given her already wealthy background, she had no need for all of the Onassis fortune, most of which went to his daughter.

Chapter 9: Ted Becomes Patriarch but not President, 1968 - 1980

Chappaquiddick

Bobby's assassination obviously shook Ted's world in more ways than one. In addition to having to grieve yet again, Ted was now the sole surviving brother, and thus the de facto leader of the Kennedy family. With Joseph Sr. on the verge of death by 1968, Ted was the patriarch of the family, a position that put all eyes were on him both among the Kennedy family and the nation. While Ted would have to publicly lead the Kennedy legacy, he would also have to play father figure to the 14 young children of Bobby's and John's who were now left without their fathers.

Initially, however, Senator Kennedy did not handle his new leadership with ease. Having been the kid brother all his life and still only in his mid-30s, Kennedy's vices were still in full force, and he was notorious both for drinking and womanizing.

In the summer of 1969, Kennedy hosted a party on Chappaquiddick Island, a small island in the southeast part of Martha's Vineyard. The party was primarily for a group of women known as the "Boiler Room Girls", who lived on Martha's Vineyard and had volunteered for Bobby's presidential campaign the year before.

After the conclusion of the party, Kennedy left the party with a 28 year old woman named Mary Jo Kopechne. According to Ted, he was simply giving Kopechne a ride home around 11:15 PM. Later that evening, however, Kennedy's car veered off a bridge into tidal water, which overturned the car beneath the water. Kennedy himself escaped and later claimed he tried several times to dive under the water to save Kopechne before returning home and leaving her at the scene.

Kopechne

Later the next morning, Kennedy reported the accident to authorities, but by then it was obviously too late to save Kopechne. Besides, local police had already discovered the overturned car.

In one night, Ted had turned himself into the subject of a major scandal, and many refused to believe the version of the story Ted was giving. The accident raised several obvious questions. First, why was Kennedy in the car with Kopechne to begin with? Kennedy had a chauffeur who had brought everyone else home. Many began to suspect foul-play, and the strange situation made even more suspicious. It was public knowledge that there were marital difficulties between Kennedy and his wife, and she had not been present at the party. Worse, she was pregnant at the time of the incident.

Other questions arose as to the nature of the accident itself, mainly why and how Kennedy crashed the car. Was it purely accidental, was it intentional, or was alcohol involved? Why did he leave the scene of the accident without reporting the incident to authorities?

A sitting Senator was now responsible for the death of a 28 year old woman, naturally leading to calls for Ted to resign. After turning himself into police, however, Kennedy gave a televised statement later that evening. In it, Kennedy claimed first that his wife was unable to attend the party because of previous miscarriages; she was at home in bed during her pregnancy. Secondly, he denied any immoral conduct and said he was not driving "under the influence of liquor." He said that not reporting the incident to authorities immediately was indefensible, but he said he was confused and delirious as a result of the accident and could not remember many details. He blamed his actions on cerebral shock. Finally, Kennedy brought a much-speculated concept out into the open: "whether some awful curse did hang over all the Kennedys."

Knowing his political career was now weighing in the balance, Kennedy asked the people of Massachusetts whether they thought he should remain in the U.S. Senate despite his behavior. After receiving a positive response, Kennedy chose not to resign. Kennedy would easily win reelection yet again in 1970.

However, Chappaquiddick would never simply blow over. Ted's life and career were permanently marred by the accident that night, and it would forever be fodder for political opponents. As it is, Ted probably got off lightly. An inquest and Grand Jury trial were conducted, in which Kennedy was given a suspended two-month sentence in jail, and a fine. The judge found that elements of Ted's account were not truthful and accused his negligent driving of causing Kopechne's death.

Kennedy's wife subsequently suffered a miscarriage, blaming it on the stress of Chappaquiddick.

The '70s and Presidential Speculation

Before Chappaquiddick, many speculated that Ted Kennedy would run for President against Richard Nixon in 1972. After all, that seemed the logical next step in the Democratic Party's succession of Kennedy's throughout the '60's. Chappaquiddick, however, destroyed Ted's viability as a Presidential candidate. He knew the issue would rise repeatedly, and that it helped solidify the widely-held view that, among the family, Ted was the spoiled brat who was unqualified to hold political office. He had spent nearly a decade in the Senate, but his political career and accomplishments were still nothing compared to what his brothers had achieved in the '60s.

Despite this, though, the Kennedy name held enormous appeal within the Democratic Party, which was still deeply divided after the trauma of 1968. Polls showed Kennedy leading the pack of Presidential contenders, but Ted himself remained skeptical. By May of 1972, he denied any interest in running for the Presidency, suggesting perhaps he would run at a later date.

For the time, Ted thought his efforts were best utilized in the Senate. There, he hoped to build a better reputation for himself. Rather than simply be associated with others by virtue of his last name, Ted wanted his own real accomplishments. In 1969, Kennedy had become Senate Majority Whip, a position that aims to galvanize party unity and get its members to vote certain ways on votes. That position gave him some extra influence over the affairs of the Senate, but after Chappaquiddick he lost that position.

Despite the setback, Kennedy decided to focus on issues. National health insurance on a single-payer model became an important issue to the Senator. Alongside President Nixon, who Kennedy thought was pragmatic and easy to negotiate with, the two nearly struck up a national health insurance deal. Though Nixon opposed Kennedy's single payer option, he would accept an HMO-based deal where private employers insured everyone in the country. Kennedy rejected the plan but later regretted it, later coming to view that missed opportunity as the last time the two parties were able to come close to a reasonable agreement that insured all Americans.

In foreign policy, the Irish Catholic Kennedy also focused on the troubles in Northern Ireland, his ancestral homeland. He opposed British policy there, becoming a vocal American opponent. Elsewhere, Kennedy became a supporter of international human rights, and thought such a focus ought to be central to American foreign policy.

At home, Kennedy built a reputation as an effective liberal among a sea of ineffective ones. While the tumult of the '60s had tinged American liberalism with a radical and impractical identity, Kennedy defied this, showing that liberal aims could be achieved across party lines. With that, Kennedy began to build the image of the "Lion of the Senate" that he would soon become.

The Carter Years

By 1976, many thought Kennedy had at last found his time to run for President. Not only had he built a more defining position for himself in the Senate, but the race for the Democratic nomination seemed wide open, with no clear frontrunner. Kennedy, however, opted out. Chappaquiddick was still a salient news topic, and Kennedy still thought it made him a nonviable candidate. Additionally, personal issues began to plague his family. Kennedy had repeatedly cheated on his wife, while Joan herself had become an alcoholic. Such personal issues made a Presidential run difficult, and it obviously would've opened the Kennedy family up to closer scrutiny. Ted and Joan ultimately separated in 1977, but did not divorce immediately.

In 1976, a Democrat returned to the White House for the first time in eight years. Jimmy Carter, the former Governor of Georgia, was the new President. Though he actually dovetailed off many of Ted Kennedy's themes – humanitarian foreign policy, and social democratic domestic policies – the two did not see eye to eye.

Though both favored a national healthcare plan, which had now become Ted Kennedy's hallmark issue, Carter and Kennedy were unable to legislate an agreement. Carter was endlessly concerned about the federal budget and the economy, which he thought was the only marker of his Presidential success or failure. Kennedy, on the other hand, thought the government needed to be more ambitious, and less timid. By the end of Carter's first term, Kennedy viewed Carter as a timid and ineffectual President, and the Iranian hostage crisis only reinforced the image nationally. Despite mutual dreams and a common party, Carter and Kennedy did not get along, and Carter's presidential approval ratings were foundering. Carter would later complain that his toughest opposition came from the liberal wing of his own party, which by now viewed Ted as its champion.

Running for President in 1980

After rejecting calls to run for President in 1972 and 1976, Ted Kennedy finally threw his hat into the race in 1980, which seemed like odd timing given that a Democrat was the incumbent. 12 years earlier, Ted had warned Bobby against doing the same thing, pointing out that running against an incumbent is almost always unsuccessful and actually hurts the primary winner's chances in the general election. So why would Ted do so in 1980?

The reasons for Kennedy's sudden change of heart were many and varied. Most importantly, President Carter, much like President Johnson before him, was unpopular and unlikely to be reelected. The state of the nation was poor, with inflation and rising unemployment hurting the nation's economy. With Bobby Kennedy previously setting the stage for a Kennedy to challenge an incumbent President, Ted Kennedy thought he'd follow in the footsteps of his brother and do the same. At the same time, Kennedy's decision was also prompted by polls indicating he could easily defeat Jimmy Carter. Such polls were taken in 1979, when the nation's economy was front and center.

When Kennedy officially entered the race, however, his fortunes quickly turned in response to global events. The Iranian Hostage Crisis began in late 1979, and a "rally around the flag" effect helped prop up Carter's approval rating. The Soviet invasion of Afghanistan also helped support the incumbent President, who was able to make statements on the issue. Any criticism of such statements was seen as "too political," limiting Kennedy's ability to maneuver.

Kennedy's early fumbling, however, was not entirely the product of external events. In an interview with CBS before announcing his run for President, journalist Roger Mudd asked Kennedy why he wanted to be president. After giving a rambling answer that clearly indicated he had not even thought up a coherent answer to that question, Kennedy's popularity dropped almost overnight. His fumbling response led many to suspect, as many had throughout his career, that Ted was just another Kennedy doing what Kennedy's do, and that he viewed the presidency like it was a birthright. Worse still, Chappaquiddick had reinforced to many that while John and Bobby were driven, Ted was the frat boy party animal along for the Kennedy ride. In the decades after Kennedy's embarrassing answer to that most important but simple of questions, a "Roger Mudd moment" became the phrase for a politician making an unnecessary blunder with the media.

Once voting began in 1980, Kennedy's campaign fell further behind. He lost the first-in-the-nation caucus in Iowa by a nearly 2-to-1 margin. Worse, he also lost New Hampshire, a state that neighbored his own. Not only had events and poor campaign appearances ruined his campaign, but Chappaquiddick inevitably rose to the fore, suggesting that it was a permanent stain on Kennedy's record. Catholic votes, who had previously rallied nationwide around the Kennedy's, were less warm to Ted, costing him critical delegates in states like Illinois.

Despite a rollercoaster nomination process, Carter clinched the nomination before June. By that summer, however, the Iranian Hostage Crisis had lagged on and the economy had not improved, causing Carter's approval ratings to plummet. With that, Kennedy won the last few primaries on the West Coast, despite having lost all except those in the Northeast.

Having already taken the unusual step of challenging an incumbent, Ted now took an even more unprecedented step by challenging him at the convention itself. Because of the change in Carter's approval, Kennedy vowed to bring his contest to the Democratic Convention, which he did. At the Convention, Kennedy asked to release delegates from being bound by primary results. He wanted to let them decide on their own, saying it was clear that Carter was not a viable general election candidate, and that he would sink Democratic Congressional chances in 1980. Delegates did not buy Kennedy's argument, which was a grand departure from previous precedents, and cast a majority of their votes for Carter, renominating the incumbent President for reelection.

Kennedy conceded to Carter, though the two were now not only unfriendly, but political enemies. On the floor of the convention, despite losing, Kennedy upstaged the President, giving what is widely regarded as the most passionate speech of his career. He told the audience of the need for a more liberal platform, saying "he work goes on, he cause endures, the hope still lives, and the dream shall never die." Moreover, Kennedy never tried to bind up the wounds within the party inflicted by his own candidacy, and Carter was left a fatally damaged president that Fall, losing badly to former California Governor Ronald Reagan.

President Carter

Jackie's New Job

In the mid-70s, Jackie had been widowed a second time, which makes it easy to forget that she was still only 46, a younger age than most sitting First Ladies. With seemingly much of her life still in front of her, she returned to a passion she had pursued in college, turning to a career in publishing.

Having spent most of her adult life in a world dictated by the ambitions of her husbands – first as the President's wife, and then as the wife of one of the world's richest men – Jackie now intended to live a more independent life. Upon returning to New York City, she began exploring the arts – painting, drawing and writing – and eventually decided a career as a publisher suited her perfectly.

In 1975, Jackie accepted a position as an editor with Viking Press. Though she enjoyed her time at Viking, she felt compelled to resign in 1978 after what might pass for a scandal in the publishing world. That year, Viking published a book entitled *Shall We Tell the President*, a fictional story in which Ted Kennedy is president and a plot to assassinate him was uncovered. The media, including the *New York Times*, heavily disparaged the novel, and given the subject matter it was widely assumed that Jackie had gotten it published, though that was not the case. Though the President of Viking felt it was necessary to inform her of the book's publication before it went to press, Jackie had not edited the work herself.

After Viking, Jackie moved on to Doubleday as an editor. Around that time, she also began consorting with long-time friend Maurice Tempelsman. In 1982, Tempelsman moved into Jackie's Fifth Avenue Apartment, and though the two never married, they appeared in public frequently, remaining companions for the rest of her life.

Unlike almost any other former First Lady in history, Jackie continued to be photographed endlessly throughout the 1970s and 1980s. Due in no small measure to Andy Warhol's iconic "Jackie O" images, Jackie continued to be a media darling throughout the remainder of her life.

Chapter 10: The Lion of the Senate, 1981-2009

The Reagan Years

Much as Kennedy predicted, Carter was trounced in the election of 1980, losing badly to Reagan. But the losses extended far beyond Carter. As Democrats worried, the choice of Carter as the Democratic Party's leader led to a rout further down the ballot, and for the first time in Kennedy's career, the Republicans took control of the Senate. Kennedy may have been the most important Democrat in Congress, but he was now returning to the upper house a member of the minority party.

Compounding the trauma of a Reagan Presidency, Kennedy's personal life took a turn for the worse, when he and his wife announced they were getting a divorce in 1981. Throughout the 1980s, Kennedy was involved in a few public drunkenness incidents, and was repeatedly caught chasing women. Though he was no longer married, his behavior was often seen as inappropriate, given his status as a leading U.S. Senator who was now in his 50s. People attending events at which Kennedy had to appear frequently noticed that he looked like hell and reeked of booze.

Because Reagan was such a dominant figure in American politics during the '80s, Kennedy saw his job as not to stop the President but merely to hold his agenda back. Kennedy became especially critical of Reagan's foreign policy, which included more aggressive rhetoric and postures towards the Soviets and intervention around the world. Senator Kennedy vocally opposed giving arms to the Nicaraguan Contras and American intervention in El Salvador. He also supported a nuclear freeze. On South African Apartheid, Kennedy visited the country despite opposition from the US and Apartheid government. There, he met with Desmond Tutu and Nelson Mandela's wife Winnie, while Mandela remained in jail. He secured passage of a set of anti-apartheid sanctions against the South African government, over Reagan's veto.

Among Kennedy's other legislative achievements in this era were increasing AIDS funding and halting Robert Bork's nomination to the Supreme Court. His impassioned statements on the Senate floor against Bork were crucial to blocking that nomination, and it came to be seen as one of the defining moments of his Senate career. After Kennedy's opposition to Bork, the Senate took a more active role in questioning and opposing Presidential nominees to the Supreme Court, instead of merely rubberstamping them.

George H.W. Bush's Administration

Kennedy declined to run for President in 1984 and 1988, knowing full well that his chances were even slimmer against a popular incumbent President. For the first time, Kennedy denied that he would ever seek the Presidency again, saying he was perfectly happy in the U.S. Senate and was content to build a legacy for himself there.

With that, however, Kennedy's personal life came front and center again after Reagan left office. Throughout the Presidency of George H.W. Bush, who Kennedy preferred to Reagan, the Senator from Massachusetts was caught in a series of scandals. The first came in 1989, when European paparazzi photographed the Senator having sex in public aboard a boat in the Mediterranean Sea.

In 1991, Kennedy was entangled in another sex scandal in Florida. There, he and his son Patrick and nephew William Kennedy Smith headed off to a nearby bar. Patrick and Smith each returned later with women they met at the bars. Later, one of the women alleged she was raped by William Kennedy Smith, and that Ted witnessed the rape but did nothing. This, of course, became a national scandal, though the Kennedys were later cleared of any wrongdoing. Many suspected, however, that a Kennedy was again given a pass due to privilege.

Despite the personal chaos, Kennedy achieved some significant legislation during the first Bush Presidency. Among his most important achievements was the Civil Rights Act of 1991, which expanded discrimination protections in employment. He also played a critical role in passing the Americans with Disabilities Act, which provided the first federal protections to Americans with disabilities. By working so successfully to get this legislation passed, despite the fact a Republican was president, Kennedy burnished his image as a pragmatic liberal who was effective in working across the aisle to forge agreements and ultimately move progressive legislation forward.

Cleaning Up in the '90s

George H.W. Bush was defeated in 1992 by the former Democratic Governor of Arkansas, Bill Clinton. Naturally, the return of a Democrat to the White House greatly pleased Ted.

That same year, Kennedy took giant steps in the quest to stabilize his personal life when he married Victoria Anne Reggie, a Washington-area lawyer. Together, the two worked to normalize Kennedy's personal life, and reinvigorate his political image, which had been badly damaged during the '80s. Throughout that decade, even voters in Massachusetts began to doubt Kennedy, and many considered him an embarrassing national distraction.

Vicki Kennedy

In part due to his political vulnerability, Kennedy faced the most challenging reelection campaign in 1994, against a young and well funded Republican named Mitt Romney. Romney portrayed himself as a political outsider who could bring a different kind of experience to Washington. Calling himself moderate, Romney advertised himself as a "change" candidate, implicitly labeling Kennedy the candidate of the establishment. Romney's chances were also boosted by the fact that the 25th anniversary of Chappaquiddick was coming up, and Ted's divorce to Joan was also in the news due to disputes over the divorce settlement.

Despite polls showing a close race, Kennedy pulled ahead down the stretch, helped by biting attack ads that accused Romney of flip-flopping and a now famous televised debate in which Ted's debate skills were fully on display. Kennedy won 58% of the vote on Election Day, the narrowest margin in his political history. Thereafter, Kennedy never again faced a serious opponent for reelection.

In the Senate, Kennedy made great gains throughout the '90s, reestablishing his position as a Lion of the Senate. He passed legislation authorizing the national Americorps public service program. After the midterm elections of 1994 swept Republicans into power in Congress, Kennedy was able to help parry some parts of the Republicans' Contract with America agenda. Kennedy also helped pass a raise in the minimum wage in 1996, as well as the Health Insurance Portability Act and other bills that required insurance companies to cover issues pertaining to mental health.

During the Monica Lewinsky Scandal, Kennedy provided comfort to the embattled President Clinton. Because Kennedy was not at all unfamiliar with sex scandals, he was able to bring humor to the President, helping calm his nerves. Clinton and Kennedy formed a close friendship throughout the '90s, and Kennedy was undoubtedly one of the President's closest Senate allies.

Unfortunately, the '90s closed with yet another family tragedy. On July 16, 1999, a plane piloted by nephew John F. Kennedy Jr. crashed on its way to Martha's Vineyard, a result of pilot error by John Jr. He, his wife, and his wife's sister were all killed in the crash, and it was once again left to Ted to eulogize a Kennedy. "We dared to think, in that other Irish phrase, that this John Kennedy would live to comb gray hair, with his beloved Carolyn by his side. But, like his father, he had every gift but length of years." John Jr. was the third nephew of Ted's to die in a span of 15 years.

Jackie's Death

John Jr.'s death in a plane crash was precisely what his mother had worried about when she first learned of his ambition to fly planes. As a result, John Jr. had put off flying until after his mother's death.

As it turned out, Jackie would also die relatively young. During the '80s and '90s, Jackie spent the remaining years of her life publishing and memorializing her husband, helping design both the Harvard Kennedy School of Government and the JFK Memorial Library in Massachusetts. In New York, she devoted herself to historic preservation projects, including the preservation of Grand Central Station.

In her later years, however, Jackie grew ill. Only in her early 60's, Jackie was diagnosed with non-Hodgkin's Lymphoma, a complicated form of cancer. The diagnosis came in January 1994 and was announced to the world the following month. Initially, doctors were optimistic, and with the hope of surviving Jackie quit smoking. But the cancer had spread by spring, and her prognosis became dire. Knowing her death was imminent, Jackie wanted to return home to Manhattan from the hospital on May 18, 1994.

On the evening of the following day, at 10:15 p.m., Jackie Kennedy-Onassis passed away quietly and in her sleep, surrounded by friends, family and books. In announcing her death to the outside world, son John Jr. stated, ""My mother died surrounded by her friends and her family and her books, and the people and the things that she loved. She did it in her own way, and on her own terms, and we all feel lucky for that."

Jackie's funeral was held at Saint Ignatius Loyola Church in Manhattan. Fans and well-wishers flocked to see her funeral, a funeral like no other former First Lady's. She was buried in Arlington National Cemetery, next to her late husband and two infant children.

George W. Bush's Presidency

Despite the drama of the 2000 Election, during which Kennedy had loudly supported Vice President Al Gore, Kennedy did not initially believe former Texas Governor George W. Bush would be a disastrous President. He had enjoyed working with the President's father in the late '80s and thought the father's son would be compromising and pragmatic. He was especially hopeful on issues of education reform.

The Bush-Kennedy relation peaked early, however. Its highpoint came with the signing of the No Child Left Behind Act in June 2001. Kennedy liked the bill's huge increases in education funding, and was willing to accept national testing standards in exchange for the new funding. Despite some Democratic opposition, Kennedy thought the bill was a reasonable one. Thereafter, however, Kennedy and Bush agreed on almost nothing. Kennedy even came to find fault with the implementation of the No Child Left Behind Act.

On September 11, 2001, Kennedy was meeting with First Lady Laura Bush when learning about the terrorist attacks on the Pentagon and the World Trade Center. Because two of the planes had taken off from Boston, many of the victims were from Massachusetts. Kennedy maintained strong relationships with the victims' families, and eventually secured legislation providing healthcare and mental health counseling to victims' families and survivors.

After 9/11, the Bush Administration began an era of international wars categorized under the banner of the War on Terror. At this point, Kennedy diverged significantly from President Bush. Though he supported overthrowing the Taliban in Afghanistan, Kennedy was among the most vocal opponents of the war in Iraq, calling it Bush's Vietnam. He called for an end to the war throughout his time in the Senate and throughout the Bush years.

9/11 ruined the Bush-Kennedy relationship, much as it ruined Democratic-Republican relationships nationwide. The Senator and the President were unable to see eye-to-eye on anything, including the Medicare Prescription Drug Act, which was something Kennedy would normally support.

The Return of Camelot and Illness

The year 2008 brought the world an unprecedented financial crisis, causing the incumbent President Bush and his party to rapidly lose popularity. Kennedy and the Democrats were wildly enthusiastic about the party's chances for a White House victory in 2008, after eight long years of what it considered to be destructive Bush policies. The problem for the Democrats, however, was who to choose as a nominee. The Party was caught between two seemingly great options: the experienced former First Lady and Senator from New York, Hillary Clinton, and the young and inspiring Senator from Illinois, Barack Obama.

In the years leading up to the election, it was viewed as Hillary's to lose, and given the political apparatus that had already been in place for President Clinton, the Clinton political machine would be a formidable opponent for anybody. Traditional "establishment" elements were lining up behind Clinton, while outsiders stood with Obama. Kennedy, the epitome of establishment, was widely expected to through his support to Clinton, whose husband he had built a strong relationship with a decade earlier.

On January 28th, 2008, Kennedy made a big and influential departure from expectations by endorsing Senator Obama for President of the United States. He did so by comparing Obama to his fallen brothers, implicitly comparing Obama to Camelot, the term used to describe John F. Kennedy's years in office. Ted called Obama a new generation of leader, saying the nation needed a change, and his endorsement was widely viewed as one of the most important points in the nomination process. Obama went on to win an incredibly contested nomination process and became President in November.

Before then, however, Ted suffered a seizure in March, after which he was quickly diagnosed with a malignant tumor. The 76 year old had brain cancer, and he was now facing a rather dire prognosis. Kennedy underwent brain surgery at Duke University in June, but the surgery was widely believed to only extend his life expectancy by a matter of months. Because of his illness, Kennedy assumed a private life, making few public appearances throughout 2008 and 2009. When he attended some of Obama's inaugural celebrations, he collapsed due to fatigue.

Kennedy made a few surprise appearances in the Senate, at one point helping to break a Republican filibuster of the Obama stimulus package. Though he participated little in the deliberations, the cause of his life – healthcare reform – was coming to a head in the Senate while Kennedy was dying.

Ted's Death

On August 25, 2009, Senator Edward M. Kennedy died at his home in Hyannisport, Massachusetts, ending nearly half a century of service in the United States Senate. Political leaders across the political spectrum paid homage to Senator Kennedy, one of the longest serving and most effective Senators in U.S. history. All surviving Presidents and first ladies gave a statement, and many former dignitaries offered their condolences as well.

Kennedy's funeral began in Hyannisport and moved to Boston and then Washington. His body was brought past numerous monuments important to his life, including the JFK Library and, of course, Capitol Hill.

Kennedy was buried in Arlington National Cemetery, next to his brother Robert alongside the other Kennedys buried there, which now included Bobby, John, and Jackie. His grave was marked with an identical marker to Bobby's.

Shortly after his death, the Affordable Care Act, which expanded healthcare coverage to all U.S. citizens for the first time in history, was passed. Ted died just months short of its passage. In Massachusetts, however, Kennedy's seat was later won by State Senator Scott Brown, a Republican, marking the first time since 1952 that a Republican held the "Kennedy Seat" in the Senate from Massachusetts.

Chapter 11: The Kennedys' Legacies

"America's Royal Family"

Although the Kennedys forged unique careers and left their own personal legacies, the four of them all intertwine to form a common Kennedy legacy at the same time.

The Kennedy family has been called "America's Royal Family," and the family's political history adds credence to the designation. Apart from Presidential hopefuls, the family has produced Senators, Congressman and many other office holders. From John Kennedy's election to the Senate in 1952 until Ted Kennedy's death in 2009, a Kennedy occupied a Senate seat from Massachusetts for 55 of 57 years. At least one Kennedy served in the House and Senate between 1952 and 2011, when Ted Kennedy's son Patrick left his seat as a Congressman from Rhode Island. Since 2011, no Kennedy has served in the House or Senate, but this vacancy may prove to be only a brief intermission. Robert Kennedy's grandson Joe Kennedy III is seeking a seat in Congress representing the Massachusetts 4th District, which today includes parts of John's former 10th District seat.

Other politicos abound in the Kennedy family, including Maria Shriver, former First Lady of California and ex-wife of Governor Arnold Schwarzenegger and Kathleen Kennedy, former Lieutenant Governor of Maryland and one-time candidate for Governor. John Kennedy's daughter Caroline also considered a run for US Senate from New York, but opted out.

John and Camelot

On an individual level, John's legacy will always be inextricably tied to the notion of Camelot put forth by his wife in the week after his assassination.

Even before his White House years, John and Jackie Kennedy fascinated the media and became integral parts of American popular culture. Few Presidents acquire the sort of celebrity status that Kennedy maintained, and the Kennedy family was wrapped in a sort of regality normally reserved only for untouchable stars. The continued popular fascination with the Kennedys suggests that Americans are still clamoring for the rare type of celebrity that John and Jackie embodied. Their celebrity lives on most strongly through the perpetual popular culture phenomenon widely referred to as Camelot.

Along with Jackie and their young children, Kennedy's presidency holds a unique spot in American history, an instance where the yearning for a vision departs from the reality of the years. Camelot has painted a picture of the Kennedy family and the Kennedy Presidency that has permanently shaped John's legacy. Thanks to Jackie, history would remember John Kennedy not as a slain President whose first few years were marked by a handful of stumbles, fits and starts, but for the potential John and his presidency represented and held. With that, the nation mourned the loss of great promise. The turbulence that followed in the late 1960's further compelled Americans to remember the Kennedy years as a more serene, peaceful time, and Camelot came to represent the innocence of the early part of that decade. Forever, Americans continue to ask themselves "what if?" What if John Kennedy hadn't been killed on November 22nd, 1963? Would the United States have endured the Vietnam War, and all of the other traumas that came that decade? Jackie Kennedy, the woman closest to the slain President of the United States, tried to mask over some of the ugly truths of those years by giving Americans a more potent symbol to hold onto.

With John's death, the Kennedy legacy and the idea of a Kennedy Curse both hardened. Naturally, John also affected his own family's ambitions. Just five years after his assassination, John's brother Robert took hold of the Kennedy torch and began his own run for the White House. In the summer of 1968, however, his dream was also cut short by an assassin's bullet. A little over a decade later, another Kennedy brother made a much less successful bid for the Presidency when Ted Kennedy challenged the incumbent Jimmy Carter in 1980. Throughout the past few decades, other Kennedy relations have vied for the top executive office, among them Sargent Shriver, who was the Democratic Vice Presidential nominee in 1972 and sought the party's Presidential nomination in 1976.

Bobby's Legacy

Despite having never sat in the White House himself, the modern legacy of the Kennedy Family might owe more to Bobby than to John.

Unlike John, who was reluctant in his liberalism and remained entrenched in the conservatism of the 1950s, Bobby dove headfirst into the progressivism of the 1960s. His legacy of fighting for minority rights, civil rights, the poor and the disadvantaged has come to define the Kennedy Family much more than John's political pragmatism and foreign policy of relative aggression and containment. After Bobby's death, Ted continued the Kennedy legacy in this same vein, becoming a champion for universal healthcare and expanded support for the poor. That work, though, was much more Bobby's vision than John's.

Bobby's premature death had several consequences. First, it crystallized the cultural memory of the Kennedy's as a quasi-royal family, dovetailing off of John's assassination. The two assassinations cemented the Kennedys as a family making the ultimate sacrifice in service of their country. In conjunction with that, Bobby's assassination further hardened the idea of a "Kennedy Curse." Becoming the second Kennedy in less than a decade to be assassinated, Bobby's death was preceded and followed by a series of horrible tragedies for the family, ranging from further death to alcoholism and other disasters. Bobby's death was even more unprecedented than his brother's: sitting Presidents had been assassinated before, but candidates had not been. After Bobby's assassination, Secret Service protection was extended to presidential candidates.

More than anything, Bobby's assassination created one of the great "what-ifs" in American history. While it will never be clear whether Bobby would have received the Democratic nomination over Hubert Humphrey in 1968, it is often widely assumed among Americans today that Bobby could have grabbed the nomination and defeated Richard Nixon, sparing the country over 4 more years of Vietnam and Watergate.

In another sense, Bobby's assassination served as an ugly bookend to a decade that started with young President Kennedy and his kid brother embodying so much potential and idealism. The decade began with the attractive Kennedy family entering the White House, and anything seemed possible. The Kennedy years were fondly and famously labeled "Camelot," by Jackie herself, suggesting an almost mythical quality about the young President and his family.

Eventually, the 1960s came to be known for their turmoil, with the optimism of the Kennedy presidency shattered by his assassination, and then Vietnam. By the time Bobby and Martin Luther King, Jr. were assassinated in the span of two months, and riots overtook the Democratic National Convention in Chicago, the country was irreversibly jaded. At the end of 1968, after Apollo 8 carried the first astronauts around the Moon and back, Astronaut Frank Borman later received a telegram from one citizen that simply said, "Thank you Apollo 8. You saved 1968."

The 1960s forced young people to come of age more quickly than ever, and Bobby seemed to be one of them. As a man who came to champion human rights and provide a voice for oppressed across the country and indeed the world, Bobby continues to represent one of America's strongest liberal voices, a mantle carried on for another 40 years by his brother Ted.

While never as glamorous as John, Bobby remained part of the Camelot narrative. Cut down in his prime, Bobby also continues to represent untapped potential and what-ifs, never given the chance to potentially let supporters down or fail to live up to his promise. Indeed, when Barack Obama barnstormed across the country like a rock star in 2008, producing adulation that literally made supporters faint, many couldn't help but compare the hope Obama inspired among supporters with Bobby's all too short campaign 40 years earlier.

Given that legacy, Bobby was one of the defining figures of the '60s, and his death was one of the decade's defining events. It would be impossible to make sense of the era without him.

Ted's Legacy

In 2010, for the first time in nearly 65 years, there was no Kennedy in Congress. That incredible streak owes almost two thirds of its existence to the kid brother, Ted. Thus, in more ways than one, Ted Kennedy's legacy has come to be the last piece of the puzzle for all of the Kennedy brothers. Each contributed something significant to the Kennedy brand. John was the pragmatic statesman, Bobby the idealistic dreamer, and Ted the legislative doer.

Although never viewed as having the potential or capacity of his older brothers, a view shared even within his family, Ted arguably accomplished more than either of them. Despite frequently being overshadowed by the two during the first half of his life, Ted Kennedy secured significant legislative accomplishments throughout his time in the Senate. The scope of his 46 years in the Senate obviously dwarfs his other brothers combined. John had been a Congressman for 14 years before serving as president for about three years, and Bobby's political experience included being his brother's Attorney General for nearly three years and serving nearly four years in the Senate. John's political career and Bobby's political career combined were barely half the length of Ted's.

While Ted will probably never have the same kind of mystique associated with his legacy, in some sense he normalizes the Kennedy brand and makes it more real. Camelot is about what may have been, but Ted's legacy is about what actually happened. In the same vein, while John and Bobby's philandering are often overlooked or even accepted as part of being a Kennedy, Ted actually had to live with the public scandals created by those vices. Through Chappaquiddick and the scandals of the 80's, Ted carried all the weight of the moral failings. For some, Ted's handling of scandals that represented vices shared by all the brothers helped make the Kennedy legacy less fairy tale and more real, reminding people that all three brothers were once mere mortals.

While Ted was the last of the Kennedy brothers to die, his legacy lives on not only through his family but through his political party. Though John and Bobby gave the Democratic Party its words and rhetoric, Ted gave it substance. Ted brought the Democratic Party platform to new heights, putting it into action like none of his predecessors. He left an enduring legacy of his own in the U.S. Senate, and for that, Ted Kennedy is duly admired.

Jackie's Legacy

As a First Lady, Jackie Kennedy outpaced her husband compared to her predecessors. More popular than the president during the Kennedy years, Jackie has gone down in history as among the greatest and most influential of First Ladies. Even today, Jackie still draws considerable interest; in conjunction with the release of a book about her, audiotapes of an interview Jackie gave to Kennedy historian Arthur Schlesinger Jr. were released in September 2011. The tapes displayed the more private side of Jackie, the intellectual woman with strong opinions. In the nearly 9 hours worth of recordings, Jackie offered more personal (and controversial) opinions on public figures of the time, including Lyndon Johnson and Martin Luther King, while offering further intimate details of life in the White House. Regardless of the merits of her opinions, it was clear she held nuanced ones.

Unlike the Presidency, the role of First Lady is a varied and malleable one. Some, like Eleanor Roosevelt, become famous for striking a philanthropic, charitable and advocacy role. Others, like Hillary Clinton, morph into quasi-Presidents themselves, and in Clinton's case, eventually go on to seek the White House.

Most, however, prefer to be the President's closest and most personal advisor. The "traditional" role of First Lady is that of wife. Most prefer to host guests in the White House and provide a stable base for the President at the end of the day. For the public, they bring out the President's softer side.

It is in this traditional role – the role still taken by most First Ladies – that Jackie Kennedy outshines all of her predecessors and successors. Jackie brought a sense of luxury, class and beauty to the role of First Lady, and while subsequent first ladies like Michelle Obama have earned praise for being fashionable and playing a similar role in her time as First Lady, none have proven as popular as the woman who blazed that trail.

Jackie's work in the White House itself, while often overlooked, was also of enormous importance. Without Jackie Kennedy, the White House the world knows today would not be the dignified and powerful building it is. Jackie made enormous inroads in ensuring that the White House was recognized as an historic monument in itself, not just an office and temporary living quarters for the First Family. She ensured that the historic treasures held within the White House walls were not hauled away by departing Presidents and made sure that the then-decrepit building was restored to its former majesty. Better yet, she did so mostly of her own accord, without funding from tax dollars.

Though she will always be tied to her husband and his presidency, Jackie's legacy stands strong aside from that. Her fashion and luxury have remained unmatched by First Ladies since, and her sense of class reinforced the narrative of the Royal Kennedys, adding unprecedented stateliness to the First Family. From Jackie onward, the First Family – not just the President himself – have become symbols for national leadership. Jackie's enormous appeal to the American public owes much to this trend.

Always a patron of the arts, Jackie offered Americans much art herself. From her dazzling style to famous photos to Andy Warhol's beloved prints, Jackie has in some ways come to symbolize her times. Jackie's life – the innocence, the class and the tragedy – serve as an historical metaphor for the transition from the content '50s to the turbulent '60s.

Indeed, Jackie's legacy was visible from afar. Lady Jeanne Campbell put it best, writing for *The London Evening Standard*, "Jacqueline Kennedy has given the American people...one thing they have always lacked: Majesty."

Printed in Great Britain
by Amazon.co.uk, Ltd.,
Marston Gate.